Oh, Solo mia!

The Hip Chick's Guide to Fun for One

wendy burt and erin kindberg

CB
CONTEMPORARY BOOKS

Library of Congress Cataloging-in-Publication Data

Burt, Wendy.
  Oh, solo mia! : the hip chick's guide to fun for one / Wendy Burt and
Erin Kindberg.
      p.   cm.
  ISBN 0-8092-9782-5
  1. Single women—Recreation.   2. Leisure.   3. Recreation.
I. Kindberg, Erin.   II. Title.
GV183.B87   2000
790.1'94—dc21   00-59013
                                                           CIP

Cover and interior design by Jennifer Locke
Cover illustration copyright © Mary Lynn Blasutta

Published by Contemporary Books
A division of The McGraw-Hill Companies
4255 West Touhy Avenue, Lincolnwood (Chicago), Illinois 60712-1975 U.S.A.
Printed in the United States of America
International Standard Book Number: 0-8092-9782-5
01 02 03 04 05 06 QM 18 17 16 15 14 13 12 11 10 9 8 7 6 5 4 3 2 1

To Deidre, Denise, and Katherine for believing in newbies
To Dad, for sharing your 30+ years of writing wisdom
To Mom, for bringing home the (meatless) bacon for 30+ years
To Aaron, for staying with me despite my writing
To Spike, for forcing me to dream outside the box
To the Just CAWS crows, for all your support—

   Do you want my autograph?

—Wendy

To Deidre Knight and everyone at NTC/Contemporary for giving
   us a chance
To Adam and Thor for everything
To Mom and Mike for their support and for always asking, "How's
   the book coming?"
To my friends and family for their encouragement
To Antonette DeLauro, who always told me I could do anything I
   wanted with writing

—Erin

Contents

Introduction

As single women, the world is our oyster. So why do so many of us end up sitting home on Saturday nights watching reruns of "Walker, Texas Ranger" rather than taking on the town?

Sure, you're a bold, independent, twenty-first-century kinda chick. You're assertive and modern, and you take pride in doing your own thing without answering to anyone. But deep down, you may have uncertainties about stepping out on a solo adventure:

> "I'd feel stupid sitting at a bar or in a restaurant by myself. Everyone else is paired up with a date or friends, and I'd be there alone."
> "I see other women out solo, but they're probably a lot bolder than me—I'm not that gutsy!"
> "Going out alone isn't as fun as it is with someone along."
> "Why get all dressed up to go out when I can sit here creating a permanent crater in this couch cushion, cradling the remote?"

We understand completely. From love seats to tandem bikes to double-occupancy hotel rooms, sometimes it seems like the whole universe is plotting to pair people up. Still, why should that mean that you have to have a pal or a date in tow to have a good time? As a smart, savvy, single chick, the world is yours. So don't wait for that phone to ring—pick a few ideas and head out for an escapade with the only friend you really need to have a good time: you!

We've compiled more than 100 ideas and inspirations to blast your butt off that couch and launch you into solo excursions ranging from mild to wild. We've included the widest possible range of activities to suit single chicks of every disposition. Whether you're a mellow bookworm type, a rugged outdoorswoman, a big-city sophisticate, or a small-town girl, we've got you covered.

To keep you on your toes, we pulled a couple of items from out of left field and mixed them in with the more mainstream suggestions. Sure, you've considered learning Spanish or joining a book club, but how about attending a Native American sweat lodge, panning for gold, spying on Area 51, or crashing a posh wedding reception? And we made it easy on you. The end of each chapter gives you great ways to get started on your solo adventure. So now you have no excuses!

Never again will you be sitting at home on a Saturday night thinking, "Hmmm . . . I feel like going out but I can't think of a *single* thing to do." If you try just one idea from this book every week, we'll keep you busy for the next two years. In fact, try every idea in this book—we dare you! And be sure to drop us a postcard from the roadside while you're out on your hip chick trip.

You go, girl!

It Ain't Over Till the Beautifully Full-Figured Lady Sings

Sign up for a singing lesson and then head out for karaoke night at your favorite pub.

Just because you were the only kid in the high school chorus asked to lip sync doesn't mean you're prohibited from ever singing again. Surely someone with an ear for music can appreciate your shower rendition of "99 Luftballons." Besides, it's not as if anyone's ever told you to stay home from the church's Christmas Eve caroling session. They just insist you are the perfect person to head up the snack committee because you make the "World's Best Cup of Instant Hot Cocoa." But even so, it couldn't hurt to take a singing lesson. Even Pavarotti practices.

So, let's say you've taken a few lessons. You've learned your scales and mastered a few simple tunes, and you've finally achieved near-divadom. Now it's time to put your money where your mouth is.

You're probably still a hair short of trying out for *Les Miserables*, and several facial hairs short of a barbershop quartet, but there is one place where you're sure to get a welcome among the other nightingales, even if it is for their own tawdry amusement.

Local karaoke bars offer much more than drunken renditions of Jimmy Buffett's "Margaritaville." For many, sharing the spotlight with other Madonna wannabes offers the support and understanding so rarely provided by vocally talented friends. (You know the ones. They could fill in for an under-the-weather Natalie

> "You don't get harmony when everybody sings the same note."
> —Doug Floyd

Merchant without disappointing a single fan.) Unlike a more formal talent show, karaoke provides all the exciting, fun atmosphere of a three-ring circus: the training ring of a shot-lined table, where the trapeze artist mentally prepares herself for her death-defying stunt by downing several doses of courage-building tequila; the main ring of the stage, where she performs her suicidal act; and the safety ring of the bar, to which she can quickly retreat should she need to console herself with what remains in the tequila bottle.

Seriously though, what have you got to lose? Realistically you can probably look forward to a few free drinks either way, congratulatory or consoling. And to gain? Self-respect? Most definitely. Self-esteem? Most likely. Notoriety? Don't count on it. But who knows? Maybe you'll be able to brag to all your friends. Maybe you'll be able to write to that cute chorus teacher, extolling the virtues of your newly developed talent. And just maybe, if someone from your church happens to be in attendance, you'll be able to spend Christmas Eve drinking someone else's hot cocoa.

 Ladies, Start Your Engines!

✳ Check your local yellow pages under singing lessons or music stores. Although not all music stores offer singing lessons, they may be able to recommend some that do.

✳ Call local high school and college music departments to ask if one of their teachers or professors gives private lessons.

✳ Contact piano stores to see if their piano instructors also teach singing.

✳ Ask a local diva who sings regularly at your favorite jazz club to mentor you.

✳ Check out singing lessons on tape at bookstores or the library.

How Much Is That Doggie in the Window?

Volunteer at your local pound—just be prepared to bring home a pooch!

It's amazing that there are actually people in the world who don't like animals.

Sure, rabbits smell and snakes are generally regarded as creepy, crawly, and overall bad company, but cats and dogs? Except when given by your overweight, alcoholic Uncle Johnnie, a sloppy, wet kiss is an endearing sign of love and loyalty. And don't even get started on the bright, oversize puppy eyes, floppy ears, and soft, plush fur. Surely the staff at the Humane Society goes crazy from all the cuteness. How could one possibly stay sane with so much unselfish love crammed into a few small kennels?

Unfortunately, in most cases that love goes unrequited, as the employees at such facilities are normally overworked and underpaid due to lack of funding. Despite the well-intentioned efforts of the on-site dog and cat lovers, many of the animals are provided with only the life-sustaining basics: food, water, and shelter. Although some do get a few moments out of their pens for brief runs or introductions to potential adoptive families, more often than not they're confined to their space for the duration of their stay.

Enter a well-meaning, good-intentioned, all-around heart-of-gold animal lover—namely, you.

> "The more I see of men, the more I like dogs."
> —Madame de Staël, 1766–1817, French social leader

Volunteer to help out at your local pound and you're sure to be rewarded with more love than money can buy. Even a few hours a month can make the difference in the life of an otherwise-love-starved animal. From filling water bowls to scratching behind the ears, your help is sure to be appreciated by the staff as well as the dogs and cats.

If you're one of the unfortunate few who has a soft spot for animals but a hard time inhaling fur balls, you can still work around the allergy dilemma by raising money to help fund the organization's rescue endeavors. Call the shelter nearest you and ask about off-site volunteer opportunities. Telethons, mailers, and bake sales can all help keep the shelter's finances above board without putting you under the weather.

However, if you choose to volunteer on-site, you might feel the urge to adopt. Your biological clock might not tick for a human baby, but a furry feline or playful pup may be another story altogether. Just be sure to come prepared; you may want to bring your checkbook. Not all shelters take American Express and you can bet none of the cuddly creatures seeking a place to call home will take "no" for an answer.

 Ladies, Start Your Engines!

❋ If you have children younger than six at home, get a dog or cat that's at least four months old. Young children may mishandle animals, causing injury to the child or the pet.

❋ If you're renting, make sure you're clear about what your lease allows. If you can only have dogs under twenty pounds, remember that a ten-pound puppy won't stay small for long.

❋ Don't ever adopt an animal with the intention to give it as a gift. The recipient may not be able to keep the pet, and that puts both of you in a tough position.

❋ Be sure to spay or neuter your pet to help control overpopulation.

❋ Get advice from the experts at the Humane Society of the United States from their website at www.hsus.org.

3

If You Can't Stand the Heat . . .

Take a cooking class with the pros.
(No, Chef Boyardee doesn't count.)

So Betty Crocker you're not. But who cares? You're perfectly happy living on ramen noodles, chocolate chip cookie dough, and diet Coke. TV dinners mean no dishes to wash, and besides, it's not like you have two sets of anything for entertaining.

Still, there's a part of you that feels like you're missing something (besides your U.S.RDA of vitamins and minerals). Sure, you're a '90s woman, and you're definitely not your mother, but just because a woman's place isn't in the kitchen doesn't mean you can't step foot in there.

In addition to the nutritional benefits of preparing a balanced meal, learning to cook can be empowering, relaxing, creative, and, yes, even fun. Imagine a class where your homework assignment is to make a chocolate layer cake with caramel frosting and raspberry filling. And where else besides a cooking class can you make a mess in someone else's kitchen without feeling guilty? Not to mention that your friends will be most impressed that you can run a company, change the oil in your car on your own, and still find the time to cook a mean chicken parmesan. Who knows? You may even become a hot commodity on this year's party circuit. After all, who wouldn't invite Martha Stewart and her world-famous lemon bars?

OK, so you're already on the A list for your charming demeanor and wry

> "My favorite thing to make for dinner is reservations."
> —Julia Child

wit. But consider the benefits that cooking has to offer your reputation as nurturer, caregiver, and overall World's Best Nonhabit-Wearing Martyr. You may not see a need for it now, but when your snooty neighbor drops by unexpectedly (as usual), wreaking of Chanel No. 5 and crying about how her cheeseball husband left her for Gennyfir the babysitter, you might help her forget about those first-runner-up beauty pageant trophies with a batch of pesto mostaccioli, followed by a slightly chilled tiramisu. ("Oh, this? It's just something I threw together.")

Just remember, unlike your Monday morning biology lab in college, taking a cooking class will probably be both fun and easy. You'll meet new people and sample great food, and it could be the one time in your life when your teacher actually believes you when you say, "The dog ate my homework."

 Ladies, Start Your Engines!

✳ Browse your local yellow pages for cooking and culinary schools that offer weekly classes or short courses for beginners.

✳ Check out bulletin boards at local bakeries, health-food stores, and kitchenware shops for free or inexpensive classes.

✳ Ask your culinary-savvy friends and family members for some good recipes. Or spend a day in their kitchens watching the masters at work.

✳ Check the lifestyles section of your local paper for articles on cooking. Many will list local businesses for more information.

✳ Taste of America provides great information on a variety of culinary subjects, including the ABCs of cooking. Their website is www.tasteofamerica.com.

✳ Use Culinary Net to search for a cooking class near you. The Web address is www.culinary.net, which includes the cooking basics.

✳ Co-op Cooking is a website where you can learn how to cook and swap meals with friends and family. The address is http://co-opcooking.com.

✳ Check out Culinary Café Chat where you can talk to beginners and pros on-line about cooking. This site is also great for recipes and more starter tips. Website: www.culinarycafe.com.

4

Second Base on the First Night

Take some advice from the Village People: it's fun to stay at the YMCA.
Well, not exactly to *stay* there, but at least to use its facilities.

Your local YMCA, YWCA, or equivalent community recreation center can provide a great place not only to let off steam and get exercise but also to make new friends. Why not join an adult intramural sports team? Learn to spike with the cream of the volleyball crop or join a softball team and get to second base without the morning-after guilt.

From the WNBA to the U.S. Women's Soccer Team, women in sports are more popular than ever. If your idea of sports used to be making out under the bleachers at a high school football game, now you can understand all the hype around actively participating. Joining a women's sports team will help build your confidence, keep you in shape, and add a little excitement to an otherwise work-consumed life. Sure, you'll get sweaty, and yeah, you may be out of shape, but who cares?

If you don't see your ideal sport posted on the bulletin board at the gym, why not start your own team? Here are a few ideas:

* Feeling slap happy? Consider an indoor floor hockey team.
* Love to skate? Opt for the on-ice version.
* Feeling silly? How 'bout the lighter version of volleyball, wallyball.

> "A pint of sweat saves a gallon of blood."
>
> —General George S. Patton

Check with the facility director and schedule a trial run.

Whether you join or form a team, be prepared for a wide range of characters. Some of the women will just be seeking a bit of R&R, but others may take themselves, and the game, more seriously. If nothing else, you'll be able to count on at least one woman who will try to steal the show. (You'll know her when you see her. She'll be the first to volunteer for the position of team captain or organizer for the league.) Inside she may be all heart with issues of low self-esteem or a need to control others, but don't count on trivial chitchat at the first game.

As for the rest of the team, you'll probably encounter some kindred spirits, playing more for fun and stress relief than a need to fill a teenage void caused by being cut from the first string varsity at age sixteen. Like you, these women will welcome camaraderie, play for fun as opposed to playing to win, and look forward to the sideline chats as much as the on-court competition.

A word of caution: Wear the proper equipment. A helmet for softball, knee pads for volleyball, and high-top sneakers for basketball (for full ankle support). If you think your life is stressful now, imagine trying to get through your day in a knee brace or ankle cast. One advantage to playing sports as an adult is that you don't have to worry about looking cool among your peers. Like you, most of them have outgrown feelings of invincibility. So wear the face mask—you'll need your teeth to chew the fat on the sidelines.

 Ladies, Start Your Engines!

✳ Don't be afraid to alternate sports to keep things lively. Bored with softball? Try tennis, soccer, softball, field hockey, aquatics, gymnastics, or volleyball.

✳ Call your local Parks and Recreation Department to get more information on women's (or co-ed) intramural sports.

✳ Check out the official YMCA website at www.ymca.org or their female counterpart, the YWCA: www.ywca.org.

✳ Stay up on the latest news about women's sports by reading any of numerous magazines dedicated to women's sports, fitness, and athletics.

5

Gone with the Wind

Frankly, my dear, you won't give a damn about anything while you're parasailing.

If you want to experience the thrill of skydiving, but you're not quite ready to parachute at 4,000 feet above a long stretch of solid earth, why not work your way up? Parasailing offers the perfect compromise: the feel of the wind through your hair without the fear of falling to your death. Sure, it's still a long drop to the water, but you have more control over how high you go than that time you jumped off a 100-foot cliff in Hawaii. Of course, you were nineteen then, and much more brave (if that's the word for it).

Remember how much you loved your vacation on the coast? Yes, yes, the locals were gorgeous, but so was the ocean. It was warm and clear enough that you could see for yourself the entirely separate world that lives underwater. Parasailing will allow you to check out that world again, this time from the air. From dolphins and ducks to reefs and fish (and hunks in trunks), you'll be able to see water life in all forms, with the variety limited only by your choice of water venue.

With the exception of getting an exaggerated wedgie from the safety harness that fits between your legs, parasailing is relatively safe. You'll be gliding over water, pulled by a boat close enough to view your hand signals indicating your suggestions—speed up, slow down, get the champagne ready, and so on.

As for training, there's not much. The instructor will probably go over

> "Life is either a daring adventure or nothing at all."
> **—Helen Keller**

some basics on the ground, including how fast you'll be going, what signals to give, and how long you'll be up in the air.

Expect to take off either from the beach with a running start or from the boat deck with a hydraulic launch and a gentle liftoff. You don't have to be particularly fit, but knowing how to swim is most definitely a benefit. You won't need to use the breast stroke, but with a beach lift off, you will get your legs wet as you run into the surf. On the upside, you'll look like an advertisement for suntan lotion. With a hydraulic launch and recovery system right from the deck of the boat, you probably won't get wet at all.

If you're still unsure about whether you want to try parasailing, ask to watch a few runs. You'll get an idea of what it's like and may be able to interview a few other first-timers to find out how the actual experience compared to their fears and expectations. Best of all, you'll know if the day's weather is conducive to the sport. If advanced parasailers are having trouble controlling their chutes, you probably want to wait for a day with less wind. You can always pop open that champagne and take in the beauty of the water from the safety of the shoreline.

 Ladies, Start Your Engines!

✳ Check your yellow pages under *watersports* or *recreation* to find a nearby business that offers parasailing.

✳ Can't find anything near you? Consider a short trip to a city famous for its water sports such as Fort Lauderdale, Lake Tahoe, or Honolulu. Make a whole day of it. Many companies will offer a discount if you parasail more than once in one day.

✳ You can expect a typical ten-minute ride to cost about $25.00.

6

The Agony of the Feet

It looks easy enough. Just strap a couple of oversize tennis rackets to your feet and trudge along in the snow in search of the Abominable Snowman. No big deal, right? Sure, if you're a Norwegian Olympic gold-medalist cross-country skier.

OK, that may be an exaggeration. In reality, almost anyone who can walk without a cane can snowshoe. But it's harder than it looks. The difficulty comes more from strength and endurance than from balance, which is the challenge with other winter sports such as skiing or ice skating. The first few steps seem relatively painless, even exhilarating, but after a few hundred steps, you begin to see why you don't see little old ladies snowshoeing to the grocery store.

As with any challenging sport, snowshoeing has its advantages: namely, it's *fun*. What other sport allows you to hike on top of five feet of snow without falling in up to your neck? And what better way to build beautiful calves and get aerobic exercise outside without pounding the pavement in $90 sneakers?

Another upside is that snowshoeing is inexpensive. You will probably spend $10 to rent a pair for an entire day. Not that you'd actually want to spend twelve hours traipsing around through snowbanks, but with the price of a movie ticket going for about the same rate, why not skip the theater in lieu of a good workout in the great outdoors?

> "The biggest sin is sitting on your ass."
> —Florence Kennedy

Finally, of all the winter sports around today, what could possibly be safer than snowshoeing? Extreme skiing? If you think that's safe, you've never seen those *Agony of Defeat* bloopers. Snowmobiling? Ever think about what happens if you run out of gas in the middle of nowhere? Ice skating? Does the name "Nancy Kerrigan" ring a bell? With the exception of an avalanche or perhaps getting lost in the woods, snowshoeing is about as safe as it gets.

Prepare for your trek as if you were going for a walk in cold weather: warm clothing, gloves, hat, and scarf. For a longer walk, wear a fanny pack to hold a map, compass, sunscreen, and an extra pair of socks. And wear lots of layers. Though it may be subzero temperatures when you start out, you're sure to work up a sweat once you get moving.

Ask the rental shop for a clearly marked trail map and stick to one trail. Don't venture into the woods or down a back road, and head back to your car before dusk, sooner if the weather starts to get bad.

One word of caution: Use a stick to poke through the snow as you walk to measure its depth. Some hard bodies even choose to use ski poles to get an upper-body workout. If the snow gets too deep to measure, turn back and find another trail. If the strap breaks on your gear, you'll have a tough time maneuvering through waist-deep snow. You don't want to become a human snowball on your first adventure, although word has it that the Yeti is looking for a mate . . .

 Ladies, Start Your Engines!

✳ Wear running shoes to hike in dry snow, hiking boots for strolling or walking through slushy snow.

✳ Choose the smallest and lightest snowshoes to support you. You certainly don't need your shoes to weigh your feet down—that's the snow's job!

✳ Wear a longer waterproof jacket in slushy snow as you'll probably kick up snow as you walk.

✳ Lead with your heel down for the most efficient gait and the best traction.

✳ Showshoes are made of many types of material. Try on a few different pairs to get the most comfortable set for your hike.

7

If I Had a Hammer, I'd Use It for Good, Not Evil

Help build houses with Habitat for Humanity.

You don't have to be an architect to build bridges in your community. Plenty of unskilled laborers have joined the ranks of construction apprentices only to graduate to the high post of Almighty Not-Quite-as-Unskilled-Anymore Laborer, thanks to Habitat for Humanity. **13**

If you've never heard of it, the world-renowned Christian-affiliated endeavor accepts volunteers from all over the globe to build and rehabilitate houses for low-income families. The program constructs simple, decent homes using volunteer labor and tax-deductible donations of money and materials.

There are two types of short-term missions available to volunteers: the U.S./Canada missions and international missions. Both offer a chance to learn about cultural differences, poverty housing, and development challenges, as well as how long you can stand living without your satin sheets and Internet access. With a balance of work, recreational activities, and free time, volunteers not only develop new housing for those in need, they build new friendships as well.

Volunteer stints start at around two weeks, during which you're expected to pay all your own expenses. But before you hyperventilate thinking about the cost, ponder the long-term savings. With affiliations in more than sixty countries, you can travel all over the globe for much less than normal. Plus, unlike your taste in clothes or music, which changes

> "Many hands make light work."
> —John Heywood

every year, your photos and stories will truly be timeless. You're investing in memories, for you and those whose homes you help create.

With per-person cost estimates running as high as $3,500 (for projects in Africa for example), most participants can't cough up the cash overnight. Many engage in fund-raising campaigns not only to fund their trip but also to raise awareness on the subjects of poverty and missions.

If covering your own costs seems impossible, consider getting volunteer and financial support through your family, friends, place of worship, or other civic clubs. You can also contact Habitat for Humanity for ideas on how to raise money. (Don't worry, they won't make you sell your record collection.)

Be prepared: This program isn't for the timid or faint of heart. You'll be working hard and will be about as far removed from pampered as you can get. Don't look for upscale hotels, gourmet meals, first-class airfare, or cable TV. You won't be sitting in the lap of luxury, but after two straight weeks of building a house for a family that really needs it, you may just feel like you're sitting on top of the world.

 Ladies, Start Your Engines!

✳ Learn what Habitat for Humanity is all about at www.habitat.org.

✳ For the Web-challenged, write or call to request a brochure:

> Habitat for Humanity International
> 121 Habitat Street
> Americus, GA 31709-3498
> (912) 924-6935

8

Just Call Me Amelia

Learn how to handle the big stick—take a flying lesson.

You may have seen them on TV, those crazy people who conquer their fears by tackling them head first. The woman who's petrified of snakes allows a boa to droop across her shoulders; the man who's afraid of water takes swimming lessons; and the kid with claustrophobia takes a trip through a network of caves. Sure, they may seem nuts, but you can't blame them for trying to conquer their phobias. In fact, you might want to put down the remote and give it a try.

Take flying for example. What better way to address your fear of 747s than learning to fly? Well, you won't actually be piloting a Boeing, but why not get behind the stick of a miniplane the size of, say, a crop duster?

One thing to keep in mind is that, for a very long time, you won't actually be flying the plane. And when you do fly, the first few times you won't be flying alone. You'll have a trained pilot right next to you, straddling a back-up stick. If at any time you feel out of control, you can signal the pilot sitting less than a foot away. You might not even need to say anything; the beads of sweat running down your face may be enough to tell the instructor to jump in.

Depending on where you live and what your goals are—a single flight or obtaining your full pilot's license—prices for classes can vary greatly. If you're just interested in trying one flight, you'll

> **"Does not enable user to fly."**
> —Warning on Batman cape

probably be looking at thirty-five to forty-five minutes of air time. You will learn some basic preflight and taxi procedures, as well as some in-flight maneuvers. And you'll be assigned your own certified flight instructor who might even let you talk to the control tower, if there is one.

If you really enjoy flying and want to get your pilot's license, you'll be paying for a lot more classes. Expect to have several classes on the ground to cover operations and systems, navigation, meteorology, and federal regulations. For extensive flying, a physical will also be necessary to rule out high blood pressure, severe vision problems, or chronic loss of bowel control due to being "really friggin' scared."

Check the yellow pages under *schools, flying,* or *airplane,* or call your local airport to find out where you can take classes. Be sure to check out your instructor's background, including number of years flying, number of years teaching, and safety record. Don't be embarrassed to ask for references, proof of certification, and a free set of steak knives.

Before you go, make a list of questions for your instructor.

* How many classes will you need to take?
* How many students are in the classroom, and how many are in the air?
* Should you say a prayer before your lesson?
* What type of clothing should you wear? (This one may sound silly, but the last thing you want is to have your hands shaking from the bitter cold at 30,000 feet. When in doubt, ask yourself W.W.A.W.—"What would Amelia wear?")

 Ladies, Start Your Engines!

* Ready to earn your wings? Find a flight school near you at www.studentpilot.net/indexie.html.

* If you decide to continue flying for your pilot's license, be sure to get the entire cost up front. Also, ask how many hours you'll need to log in the air and in the classroom.

* Warning: Don't flirt with the pilot! He needs all the concentration he can muster when teaching a hot, single chick to fly!

9

Can I at Least Keep the Towel On?

Hire a masseur and get spoiled in the privacy of your own home—without the morning-after guilt.

You work hard for your money and work hard to budget your money. You brown bag your lunch (on Wednesdays), you don't buy anything you don't really need (shoes don't count, right?), and you always use coupons (remember that buy one, get one free biscotti?).

With that said, why not indulge in a little bodywork? No, not the kind your mechanic did when you rear-ended that BMW. Real bodywork. Hands-on, deep-tissue, better-than-sex bodywork. The kind that makes you forget all about the pile of work on your desk while reminding you that money really *can* buy happiness: massage.

And with the ever-growing popularity of home delivery—don't deny it, the pizza boy knows you by name—why torture yourself being a stranger in a strange land? Sure, there are nice salons, but in addition to being quite costly, you could be looking at a three-week waiting list. Or worse, a two-hour wait past your scheduled appointment in a room full of outdated magazines (When was the last time Cheryl Tiegs was on the cover of *Vogue?*) because Gregory is still waxing Mrs. Abachi's mustache.

Of course, there are cheaper places, but do run-down massage parlors really conjure up images of rest and relaxation? You may want to also consider the possibility of being greeted by an overly tanned seventeen-year-old stripper named

"I went to a massage parlor. It was self-service."
—Anonymous

Ivory, who leads you to a red velvet room that smells more like a locker room than a Swedish spa.

Luckily, there is a way around both extremes: Hire a masseuse or masseur to come to your house. It's private, not as expensive as you might think (some run as low as $30 per hour), and much more conducive to getting what you envision as the perfect rubdown. You choose the music, the ambiance, and most important, the scent.

Keep in mind, however, that these men (or women) are there to work. Don't expect to get a date (or anything else) out of Sven. What can you expect? That depends. Ask questions in advance so you'll be sure to get a reputable business; a professional, licensed masseur; and the massage you want. Sven may know how to read your body, but don't assume he can read your mind.

Still feeling guilty about a little self-pampering? Balance your budget and cut out a few small unnecessaries. Do you really need two five-dollar lattes every day? And what about those nine magazine subscriptions, half of which are still in the plastic covers, sitting on your nightstand? And next time you walk by that shoe sale, take a moment to picture yourself getting a massage. Your neck, your shoulders, your calves, even your toes will be soft, relaxed, and pampered—ready for a fresh coat of bubble gum pink polish to take to your job along with a new attitude in a brand-new pair of open-toed slingbacks. On second thought, last year's sandals are still in style, so the shoes can wait. Besides, you've got a new addiction. And his name is Sven.

 Ladies, Start Your Engines!

✳ Communicate with your masseur. Like most men, he's no mind reader. Tell him if he rubs too hard or needs to focus more attention on your precious piggies.

✳ Ask for aromatherapy ahead of time or offer to provide your own favorite scented lotion or oil. Be clear on which scents you like and which make you wish you had a horrible head cold.

✳ For goodness' sake, wash your stankin' feet! If your masseuse or masseur is a hottie, you're going to be putting out enough pheromones as it is. The last thing you want to do is miss enjoying your wonderful massage because you're worried that your feet stink. And while you're at it, loofah those bunions!

10

The Money Pit

Take a Ms. Fix-it class and learn how to tile with style.

Times, they are a changin'. Today women are plumbers, electricians, and contractors—you just don't happen to be any of them. Still, with places like Home Depot and Home Base, you don't need to have a certificate on your wall to make minor, or even major, repairs and renovations.

From a downtown studio to an uptown penthouse, no one is safe from cracks, wear and tear, and an overall compelling need to redecorate. But who says you have to hire outside help? Why pay a plumber $100 an hour just to unclog your drain or spend thousands to retile a bathroom that you could do yourself for a fraction of the cost with the help of a few classes at your local home improvement store? Need to replace screen windows? Don't know when to change your furnace filters? Call to find out what classes are coming to a store near you. Workshops are usually free, as the store assumes you'll buy your materials there. Most classes are held on Saturdays and Sundays to work around a typical Monday-through-Friday, nine-to-five work schedule.

Classes vary greatly, depending on most frequently requested topics and seasonal changes, so don't expect to take a class on building a deck in early winter or replacing your hot water heater in early spring.

What can you expect? Everything from installing a new sink or yard lights

> "Not only is there no God, but try finding a plumber on Sunday."
>
> —Woody Allen

to putting up wainscoting or a decorative border. Check out the how-to clinic board at a store near you for upcoming workshops.

In addition to providing you with step-by-step instructions on various home improvement projects, the sales associates will make sure you've got the right tools and materials to begin. Don't worry about needing to make numerous trips back to the store to pick up supplies for each job. You can expect to receive a list of project necessities at the end of your workshop.

Chances are you'll have fun in the class and even more fun at home doing the project yourself. You may find that getting your hands dirty really suits you. You'll still have jobs that require a professional, but the next time the plumber bends over to expose his (or her) massive crack, you'll be armed with new-found know-how—and a pint of spackle.

 Ladies, Start Your Engines!

✳ Home Depot offers a ton of great workshops for free. Check out their website at www.homedepot.com.

✳ Not to be outdone, Home Base also offers free workshops: www.homebase.com.

✳ Don't limit yourself to just one category. Learn how to build, fix, decorate, install, or grow anything your heart desires. Learn how to do it right the first time to save money over the long haul.

11

Sex, Lies, and Videotape

Make a videotape for a friend who is far away.

With the exception of taping family reunions, recording your neighbor's kid's ballet recital, and trying to meet Bob Saget, your camcorder was a waste of money. Remember how excited you were when you first bought it, swearing on Aunt Tuti's grave that you'd use it every day, much like those pleather pants that now line the shelves in your garage? Well, you can stop feeling guilty. Your investment is about to pay off.

That long-lost friend you've been meaning to contact is about to receive the best gift you can give her: a videotape of you! Of course, ninety minutes of watching you wave to the camera may bore her into a coma so start writing your screenplay now while the iron (and the brainstorming) is hot.

Why not give her a brief tour of your city, beginning with that little place that you call home. A short walk through your place, complete with stops at poignant, personal reminders—a picture of the two of you together, strategically placed on your mantle; the figurine she gave you on your twenty-fourth birthday; your basketball jersey from your days together on the courts—are sure to send the warm fuzzies through the VCR.

Then head outside to share the view from your front yard. Or focus in on your neighbor weeding her garden

> "If you ever see me getting beaten by the police, put down the video camera and come help me."
> —Bobcat Goldthwait

as you whisper insider secrets about her fetish for younger men or how she still hasn't returned your rake.

Take a trip to your work and give your friend a glimpse of your daily life. Be sure to include an exaggerated wide-angle pan of your huge pile of paperwork with a quip about "now you see why I have no time to write—or date."

If the law allows, bring the camcorder to your local hangouts: a swank coffee house, a hot new club, your favorite bookstore. Let her see a few of the characters who make your Saturday nights fun—or remind you why you should have stayed home and read a book.

Visit a few friends or invite them over for an evening of video introductions. Have a list of funny questions to ask on camera that offer a true representation of their character. "Sara, tell us about the time you got pulled over in your bathrobe," or "Nathan, remind me again why you were banned from that pool hall." You're sure to make a splash with your hammiest friends, and you may be surprised to see the quieter ones come out of their shell on camera. Just remember to keep it clean—you never know who's going to get their hands on the video. Your pen pal may unwittingly pop it in during a visit from Mom and Dad. And even if you're sure she'll watch it alone, be on your best behavior. The post office delivers in rain, sleet, hail, and snow, but they've been known to lose things.

 Ladies, Start Your Engines!

✳ Even if you think it's dorky, use a neck strap. It takes only one case of butter fingers to ruin your day—and your camera.

✳ If you're filming people, try to catch the light on their faces, not their backs. A video full of silhouettes isn't much fun.

✳ Write a basic script or outline. Have a beginning, middle, and end, and include some spunky narration to help explain what's going on.

✳ Bring a waterproof bag in case it rains even if the sky is clear and sunny when you head out.

12

Banish the Bedpan Blues

Make a batch of homemade cards and visit the children's ward at a nearby hospital.

Think back to the third grade. The year you kissed your first boy, starred in your first play, and broke your first bone. Ah yes, the playground accident.

Now think back to your day in the emergency room. The horrible smell, the scary feeling of not knowing what to expect, the boring wait with nothing to do. Imagine that day times seven. A whole week. Or worse yet, a whole month. Such is the life of some of the children at your neighborhood hospital.

Although the thought may be enough to keep you in bed all day (OK, a "Real World" marathon is enough to keep you in bed all day), there is something you can do. Why not make a batch of homemade cards and visit the children's ward? You don't have to be a Picasso to cut, paste, and draw your way into the hearts of the little ones. Grab a stack of funnies from the Sunday paper or clip pictures of horses, toys, and monster trucks and create a collage of "happy things" with a simple get well message inside.

Ask the neighborhood kids for ideas on what's hot and what's not among the adolescent and preteen collective. Is a certain pro wrestler all the rage with the boys? Cut out his picture from a teen magazine and draw a bubble with the message, "Get well soon or I'm gonna kick your butt!" For the kids who

> "Get it right. I ain't a humanitarian—I'm a hell-raiser!"
>
> —Mary "Mother" Jones

can't read yet, position the hunk of manliness on a tricycle or dress him up in a skirt and rabbit ears. Generally, the younger the kid, the sillier the better.

For older girls, create a collage of funky clothes with a message like "Guess all that shopping at the mall really wore you out!" or a get well message coming from the mouth of a famous female athlete. For younger girls, a cuddly kitten, dancer, or acrobat will make an interesting card to brighten up her room.

Deliver the cards dressed in your best and brightest attire, and be sure to bring your most important pick-me-up, a sincere smile. The cards are only 10 percent of the visit, your presence is the other 90 percent. You're sure to brighten some faces, if only for a moment, and the visit may be just the thing you need to remind you of the things you're thankful for.

 Ladies, Start Your Engines!

✳ Recycle old cards by cutting and pasting pictures and words to make a room-brightening collage.

✳ Offer to teach a class to the kids on the ward on whatever happens to be your area of expertise, including painting, drawing, jewelry-making, or the art of feng shui.

✳ Solicit donations from local businesses to buy craft supplies: empty fabric totes and fabric markers, watercolors, glue, scissors, beads for jewelry, and more.

13

Big Brother Is Watching— That Pervert!

Get involved in local government and attend a town meeting.

Think all government-related meetings are boring? Don't be so quick
to judge. Attending a town meeting can be both interesting and beneficial, especially if you want to earn a reputation for kickin' ass for your community.

You know how sometimes you catch a glimpse of the cover of the newspaper as you stumble into the minimart for your morning coffee and snack bar? Those stories that really irk you are nudging you to follow your true calling—to slip into the nearest phone booth, don your shiny red cape, and right wrongs all over town.

What sort of wrongs need to be righted, you ask? Let's say you read that there were three car accidents in one week on the main road by your house. Maybe you're sick of seeing people get hurt, tired of driving over glass, or just plain fed up with all the rush hour traffic that's made you late for work all month. (OK, the oversleeping doesn't help either.) Attending a town meeting will give you a chance to voice your opinions and remedies for the problems that plague your daily life.

Sure, there's a chance that your taxes might go up if you keep fighting for wider roads, but on the other hand, there's a chance that they might actually go down when you find out what *else* your taxes are being spent

> "I think it's about time we voted for senators with breasts. After all, we've been voting for boobs long enough."
> —Claire Sargent

on and vocalize your disgust. ("Whatdaya mean the mayor needs a raise? He works only two days a week!")

And what about that developer who wants to come in and buy out all the houses in your neighborhood to build a supermall? The nerve! Who's going to stand up at the town hall and speak for all the folks whose voices are too feeble to be heard over the growling greedmongers? Who will tell them, "Hell, no! We won't go!" and adamantly insist that these people deserve better—that some of them have lived in the neighborhood for fifty years and can't be expected to bail out just because the developer is offering . . . oh . . . really? That much, huh? Maybe you should call a brief recess.

In any case, your vote counts as much as the vote of the fifty-year-old, white male Republican who thinks he should be able to decide what's best for you. Why give him a free ride when you can cause a stink simply by showing up and rockin' the boat?

Of course, it's possible the most exciting topic will be whether or not to fix the cracks in the sidewalk, but you can always slip out the back door and run away unscathed. However, if things do get heated up, you may find yourself slipping out of your coma and into a nomination to run for mayor. Then you could put those taxes to some *real* use: bigger phone booths.

 Ladies, Start Your Engines!

✳ Call your mayor's office to find out when the next town meeting is, and ask if you can get your name on the mailing list.

✳ If you're feeling sheepish about going alone, ask a friend or neighbor who has voiced similar concerns (about the roads, traffic, taxes, etc.) to join you.

✳ Don't be afraid to speak up about issues that affect you. Just be sure to arrive on time. If you get to the meeting late and they've already covered the issue, you might be embarrassed.

14

Will This Be on the Test?

Sneak into a college lecture and gawk at the cuties while you expand your educational horizons.

Whether you've accrued unimaginable debt in the form of student loans or opted to skip the college experience, you're at least familiar with the concept of the college seminar—an old, acoustically challenged auditorium filled with passed out partiers, wide-eyed brown nosers, and those in between, who are probably only there for the social scene.

Depending on your taste and your educational interests, you should be able to find at least one class that offers a delicate balance of tantalizing subject matter and prospective hotties. Begin by picking up a schedule of classes from a nearby state college's admissions office. (Private schools might not be as keen on strangers sitting in.) Choose the subjects that appeal to your academic palate and fit into your busy work schedule. If you're more interested in the attendees than the curriculum, you may want to think carefully about your scheduling choices. Any class before 10 A.M. is likely to be low in attendance.

First and foremost, size does matter. Pick a class that's being held in a theater or auditorium to offer the easiest means of sneaking in or out without being caught. This is not to say that you don't want to be noticed. On the contrary. Turning the heads of a few potential dates may not be so bad. Catching the eye of the professor who knows all her students by name, however, could cause a scene that you're not ready to endure.

> "I have never let my schooling interfere with my education."
>
> —Mark Twain

As for the variety of students, classes required to be taken by everyone will offer the most. Keep in mind, however, that you may encounter a room full of drooling freshmen (awake or asleep) or a bunch of superjocks sitting through their third year of Introduction to Algebra.

If it's the course material you're after, opt for a more focused class that has more to offer your intellect than your little black book. Of course, there are latent consequences to choosing American Poetry of the Nineteenth Century or The European Impressionists. You may find yourself scouting out some very cultured and intelligent fellow students.

And if you're looking for the male version of yourself, don't rule out women-centered courses. You may find yourself sitting next to a very sensitive equal-rights advocate who has no issues with his mother, no qualms about women making more money than men, no history of bad break-ups . . . and no date for Saturday night.

Even if the students seem too young, too immature, or just outright uninteresting, you can take comfort in the fact that you're learning something new without buying $500 worth of books or taking out any loans that'll keep you in debt until you retire.

There is that chance the professors will notice you, but they'll probably be so happy to have a student actually listen to them that they will let you slide—especially in a state school, which is more open to visitors. To be safe, grab a seat far enough to the back of the room that you can slip in undetected. On the other hand, you may want to grab a seat up front—especially if the professor doesn't appear to be wearing a wedding ring.

 Ladies, Start Your Engines!

✳ Take a class that could help your career advancement.

✳ Make sure the class is interesting in case there are no hotties to keep you occupied.

✳ Don't forget to eat before you go so your stomach doesn't growl loud enough to wake up the guy next to you.

Six Degrees of Separation

Join a networking group to make new friends and business contacts.

From the four-hour droning of corporate three-piece suits to the harried twenty-minute power lunch over Perrier and salad, schmoozing has equaled snoozing for way too long. It's time to take a break from the norm with the remodeled version of the round-table marketing spiel: the networking group.

These groups come in all shapes and sizes. Organized groups such as the American Business Women's Association or the National Organization for Women can offer more structured meetings, while local community businesses may offer such loose formats as chats over coffee or Valium swaps. If you're looking to meet business people of similar ethnicity or race, the Black/Hispanic/Native American Chamber of Commerce in your area may offer a weekly or monthly meeting to swap leads or just to make new friends.

Many networking groups (also called *leads groups*) are careful to allow only one person per business category (i.e., one real estate agent, one dentist, one hooker, one starving artist) to avoid conflicts when leads arise, so ask ahead of time if your field is already represented. If it is, you've got three choices: ask your contact to recommend another leads group for you to approach; consider starting your own group with friends, relatives, or members of your religious group; or bribe the current member in your field with lavish gifts.

> "The best way to predict your future is to create it."
> **—Anonymous**

If you do find a networking group that's taking new members, make sure you know all the details up front to avoid any embarrassment later. Many require you to pay yearly dues, which could run as low as $20 or as high as $200. Don't assume the cost is the same as your last group or the one your best friend is in halfway across the country. (She tends to exaggerate anyway.)

Also make sure you're clear about how frequently the group meets—weekly, monthly, or quarterly. No sense joining a group that meets once a month on the same night as your free HBO deal; likewise, if the group meets for breakfast at nine and you have to be at work at eight . . . (do the math).

Even if you're not out to get client leads, consider the opportunities you may encounter. Need a new climbing buddy? Someone to watch all your favorite chick flicks with? A link to a new job? Other benefits of joining a networking group include building knowledge and skills, hearing key speakers, getting invited to parties and events, and receiving discounts on goods and services. Networking is also helpful if you're a newcomer to the area. What better place to get recommendations on the hot clubs, best restaurants, a good dentist, a gynecologist, or swanky XXX theaters?

Still not sure if a networking group is right for you? Ask for an invitation to sit in on one, just to get the feel for things. You can always decline joining and try another one. If nothing else, you could walk away with at least one new friend, who you can meet on your all-too-short lunch break for salad and Perrier.

 Ladies, Start Your Engines!

✳ Contact your Chamber of Commerce for contact names and phone numbers for area leads groups.

✳ Check several local business newspapers for announcements and invitations.

✳ Note that most leads groups offer membership on a first-come, first-served basis for competing businesses.

✳ Warning: Many groups will revoke your membership after three "no-shows."

16

Leave-Your-Razor-at-Home Week

Go to a women's retreat for a long weekend of no makeup and loud belching.

Remember how you used to make fun of those middle-aged women who sat around in circles chanting mantras in a little rustic cabin in the woods? You mocked the idea of "getting back to nature," cringing at the thought of being stuck in a remote locale with no telephone, no TV, and no curling iron, and you couldn't *imagine* not shaving for an entire week.

Flash forward to today, when a more mature, modern, self-actualized version of your younger self daydreams of a wonderful break from your fifty-hour work week, two-hour daily commute, and underutilized "free time," a term that ranks close to *unicorn* and *leprechaun* on your Myth or Reality Top 10 List. Suddenly you realize that a women's retreat is not only a relatively inexpensive means of getting away for awhile but actually a very, very cool idea.

So you check your local artsy newspaper and find a great weekend getaway in the woods: nature walks, a private room, a hot tub, and all meals—real, home-cooked meals—prepared for you. No shopping, no prepping, no dishes. Just you sitting at the table, eating at the table, and walking away from the table. That's reason enough to get away! And feel free to leave your toiletries at home. No makeup, mousse, or hairspray needed. The only impression you'll be making is with your head on a down pillow.

> "People call me a feminist whenever I express sentiments that distinguish me from a doormat."
> —Rebecca West, 1913

But there's more. You'll have the opportunity to make new friends, share ideas, swap stories, and learn new things. From writing to belly dancing, horses to empowerment, there's a retreat out there with your name on it.

Still afraid to leave your razor at home? Consider that 1) you'll be far from civilization, and 2) you can opt for a women-only retreat. Chances are that any woman willing to venture away from home on her own for a little rest and relaxation is more concerned with drawing a hot bath than drawing conclusions about your true hair color.

Most retreats will welcome all shapes, sizes, ethnicities, religions, and sexual orientations, offering an interesting weekend, if nothing else. Be sure you know what you're getting into, however. You'll want to find a focus that fits your needs. If you just want some peace and quiet, look for a program without a schedule (other than mealtime). You're still welcome to strike up a conversation with the woman next to you at dinner—you just won't be chanting next to her in the mantra circle.

 Ladies, Start Your Engines!

* Call ahead for good directions. If there's time, request that the retreat send you a map, or ask if they have one on-line.

* Get specific details. What looks like a castle in the brochure may end up as a shack. Ask if you're sharing a room, if the beds have linens, what meals are provided, and what amenities are offered.

* Ask for the bill up front. You don't necessarily have to pay in advance, but know exactly what you'll be paying before you arrive. Be sure to ask if your deposit is nonrefundable.

* Ask what facilities are nearby and what activities are offered, such as a lake for swimming or boating, horseback riding, shopping, a hot tub, a pool, or all of the above.

* If you're going to a facilitated retreat, ask for references or credentials for the speakers and organizers.

* Pack for every season. Many retreats are in the woods and may experience weather several degrees colder than urban areas. When in doubt, pack clothes that you can layer.

How Much for That Yard Sale Sign?

Bring on the early birds with a weekend yard sale to get rid of all your spandex.

If you won't accept the reeking dog pee as a sign that it's time to get rid of your couch, at least admit that all of your exercise equipment is still in the original wrapper. And unless your personal psychic has forecasted an '80s retro movement, there's really no excuse for hanging onto all that crap you call "clothes."

With a firm veto against the making of *Flashdance II*, the legwarmers can go. And spandex? Leave something to the imagination. Besides, with the exception of bicyclists, anyone wearing spandex loses the right to make fun of fat men in Speedos—and you wouldn't want to lose that luxury.

Now that you've realized the error of your ways, it's time to plan for a major overhaul. Sure, you could give all that stuff away, but why not make a little pocket money to buy some new junk? Yard sales are a great way to pawn off useless items while relaxing in the comfort of your own front yard. Consider it a day of relaxation, not work. Plan to make some lemonade, invite your neighbors to stop by, and pull out some lawn chairs.

Concerned about what clothes to sell? Use these general rules:

* If you didn't wear it last year at this time, you won't wear it this one.
* Don't expect to lose weight to fit into clothes in storage.

> "Fashion is something that goes in one year and out the other."
> —Denise Klahn

33

* Don't wait for anything to come back in style.
* If it still has the tag on it after more than a week, sell it. You obviously weren't that excited about wearing it.

As for furniture, sell anything that's not valuable (emotionally or monetarily) that you don't use. Unless it's an antique or family heirloom, you can always buy another one. Be sure to mark your display tables and the chairs you're sitting on as "not for sale" in case a friend or neighbor makes sales for you while you're in the bathroom or grabbing a soda.

Tag jewelry carefully, especially the more expensive pieces. Let anyone helping you know in advance what jewelry is "high-end." In addition to not wanting it to walk away, you certainly don't want to come back from checking on your dog to learn that your friend sold your twenty-dollar earrings for a quarter.

With the exception of furniture, your items should be inexpensive. Yard salers expect bargains. Thrift stores use the 10 percent write-off rule, donate a $50.00 dress and get a $5.00 tax write-off. It's a good rule for yard sale items as well, depending on the quality of the item you're selling. A $10.00 toaster may sell for $1.00, a $30.00 lamp for $3.00.

Any items that have been awaiting repair or refinishing may earn you more money by attracting others with similar interests. That wooden chair that you bought for $2.00 with good intentions of repainting to match your bedroom set might sell for $4.00 to a thrifty craftsperson. Stop thinking you'll get to it eventually. It's been three years. Chances are you'll be glad to get rid of it, and if you do regret selling it, you can buy another one—at someone else's yard sale.

 Ladies, Start Your Engines!

* Get your neighbors involved to make the day or weekend a "Block Sale."

* Make plenty of signs to post around the neighborhood before the morning of the sale. Include directional arrows and your address. Just be sure to remove the signs when you're done!

✳ Price your items ahead of time with removable stickers or masking tape.

✳ Have a bunch of "useless" items in a box labeled free.

✳ Have grocery bags available for people who purchase several items.

✳ Have a power cord on hand to plug in electronic items to prove they work.

✳ Place visually appealing items near the road to attract passersby who may or may not be looking for yard sales.

✳ Keep your pets inside, in the backyard, or at a neighbor's house for the day. Even a small dog could scare off potential customers.

✳ Be sure to have plenty of change ready: singles, fives, tens, and coins.

18

Music Soothes the Savage Breast

Troll a new section of the CD store and expand your music selection.

Maybe the thought of rap music makes you cringe. Or perhaps you think all country songs are just whiny stories about tough trucks, lost dogs, and loose women set to a banjo. Whatever your thoughts, there's one thing that you can say about today's musical genres: there are a lot of them.

When your parents were growing up, they had a lot less to choose from. Today, you've got the music of your grandparents' and parents' generations, as well as your own. In the past few decades alone we've had the pleasure (and displeasure) of seeing such new categories as heavy metal, alternative, New Age, hip hop, techno, pop, rap, and Christian/"Positive" rap, not to mention the revivals of disco and swing. Why label yourself as a metalhead or pop diva when there's so much you haven't even explored? Sure, there's a time and a place for everything. Your KISS CD may keep you awake for that long road trip, but do you really want to use it for background music when you throw your first Thanksgiving party? The same goes for your collection of New Age instrumentals: they make for great study music, but getting pumped up before your big exam may require something a bit more . . . um . . . energetic.

If you're afraid of spending $15.00 on a group you've never heard of, consider a compilation CD. You've seen them on late-night TV—"Best of the '80s" or "Top

> "Anything that is too stupid to be spoken is sung."
>
> —Voltaire

100 Pop Hits of All Time." What are the chances you're not going to like *any* of the songs? Surely a collection of multiple artists is bound to hold at least a few addictive tunes.

Soundtracks also offer some great variety. Remember that movie you saw that had every song you ever loved growing up but you never knew who sang them? To find what could turn out to be the next *Grease*, skim the music store's collection of soundtrack CDs and tapes. You never know what great hits you might discover.

Another advantage that you have over the last generation is the opportunity to listen to music in the store before you buy it. Many music stores now offer headsets and CD players so you can sample before you splurge. Or, if you're on-line, check out a music site like CDnow.com and click on some samples.

If the store doesn't offer the chance to listen before you buy, ask if there's a guaranteed return policy. Some stores offer a return policy on their "suggested" CD (i.e., "If you don't like it, bring it back"). Ask a clerk to describe the music on a recommended CD to the best of his or her ability. Here are some helpful questions: Is it dance music? Whose style does the music resemble? How would you categorize the genre (country, alternative, rap)? If they do offer a no-questions-asked return policy, take advantage of it. When you get home, if you find it's not what you wanted, at least you'll know you can exchange it for something a little more to your liking.

Ahhhhhh. If only dating offered the same deal.

 Ladies, Start Your Engines!

✳ Not sure what you'll like? Listen before you buy at CDnow's website: ww.cdnow.com.

✳ Rather skip the mall? Download music at home through: http://listen.com.

19

Benji Makes House Calls

Start a monthly project of bringing animals from a shelter to a nearby nursing home.

When was the last time you were in a nursing home? Not to drop off **39**
something for your job or wait for a friend to get off work before a
night of painting the town red. Waiting in a tiny lobby watching the
Friday night lineup hardly counts as bringing some light into an older
person's world. And if you want to read outdated magazines, schedule
an appointment to get your teeth cleaned.

Talking to and spending time with older people can be a fun and
enlightening experience. Many have great stories to tell and fabulous
tidbits of wisdom to impart on those who are willing to listen. Think
of the older folks as foster grandparents and you're sure to enjoy their
friendship as if they were blood relatives—probably more!

Unlike hospital wards, you don't have to be a relative to visit a con-
valescent home. And despite a certain need for cleanliness, many nursing homes don't harbor the need for as sterile an environment. Some
even allow brief visitations with pets! Sure, bringing flowers is nice,
but why not share the joy of animals by offering to bring by a couple
of cats or small dogs? Your local Humane Society or animal shelter
will probably be more than happy to
give you a few "loaners." If you're
clear about your intentions and that
you'll be handling the animals alone,
they'll probably offer the assistance of
a trained volunteer. The volunteer

> "Great opportunities to help others
> seldom come, but small ones
> surround us every day."
> —Sally Koch

will not only help you choose the friendliest and tamest of the lot, but he or she may also help you transport and manage the pets in the nursing home.

Call ahead to find out what the home's policy is and if there's a space that would accommodate the animals. Think floor, as opposed to rug, in case you have to clean up after Fido, and keep the show as far away from the exits as possible. First-timers may want to try a short-term-care facility, at least to start. Long-term homes may have more patients with progressive illnesses, which may be tough to bear for new-comers.

Have a list of questions to double check the pound's top picks. For cats or kittens, ask if they are declawed and if the fluffier felines will shed. You don't want to spark a string of allergy attacks among the petting bonanza's attendees or spend six months trying to get the fur balls off your car's interior. As for the canines, opt for smaller, more timid pups with no history of biting or nervous barking. And just to be safe, ask if there's a chance that the dogs are in heat. You just might want to return sometime for a repeat performance, and an embarrassing leghump may ruin your chances.

 Ladies, Start Your Engines!

✳ Ask the shelter what days and dates the animals are available, then check with the nursing home to see if any of the times work.

✳ For retirement communities, ask what the pet policies are for seniors who have their own apartments. Some may or may not want to encourage seniors to actually adopt the pets that you bring.

✳ Ask the Humane Society for dogs that are less likely to cause allergies, such as short-haired or hairless dogs.

20

You Want Fries with That?

Whether your morning ritual consists of donning a paper hat or a surgical cap, your life experiences can offer an invaluable service to curious prepubescents.

Offering to speak on career day at a local school can be an enlightening event for both you and the students. Remember the days when guest speakers were rivaled only by field trips as a means to avoid class? Like that time police officers brought in samples of uppers, downers, poppers, and those little white pills your Aunt Felice kept hidden from your uncle. And what about the time the town expatriate brought in his twelve-foot python that kept your teacher standing on her chair all day?

With the exception of perhaps more women in the workforce, not much has changed since you were in school. Kids like fresh faces, new stories, and anything that doesn't require using the Pythagorean theorem.

Are you worried the story of how you started your Wiener schnitzel shop will bore everyone into a coma? Consider giving it the old college one-two and offer to give a talk about your alma mater to an older group of students, say, juniors or seniors in high school. Be sure to include all the "juicy" details (nothing that would make your mother disown you!) about moving away from home, campus food, decorating

> "Executive ability is deciding quickly and getting someone else to do the work."
>
> —John G. Pollard

your dorm room with street signs, how to get along with a roommate, the hotties on the basketball team, and the rules about dating professors, sleeping with resident assistants, and sneaking booze into your room. Be sure to focus on the good things about college. You don't want a mob of angry parents banging on your door the next day saying their kids just decided *not* to go to college.

Another possibility is to talk about a specific experience that may interest kids while sharing an important message such as a car accident involving a drunk driver, a trip to Europe, or meeting the president. Just remember, kids don't like to be preached to. Make a point but keep it light, even humorous: "Then the president's dog peed on my leg!" or "I didn't know I was eating beetle brains until the tour guide told me."

If all else fails, have a backup plan: FOOD. Chocolate to represent your trip to Switzerland, mini wieners from your catering company, or cereal packets from your job at Kellogg's. As the (slightly twisted) version of the old adage goes, the way to a kid's heart is through his stomach. Besides, no one can resist a speaker who brings food *and* gets them out of algebra.

 Ladies, Start Your Engines!

❊ Make sure you prepare age-appropriate material to maintain the interests of the students.

❊ Dress the part. Don't fool the kids into thinking that all CEOs get to work in jeans and dirty sneakers!

❊ If you're looking for interns, bring some business cards. High school seniors usually work cheap or for free and can often bring fresh ideas to your company.

21

Thou Shalt Not Covet Thy Neighbor's Newspaper

Bake a batch of chocolate chip cookies for that neighbor you've never really met.

If you're still referring to your neighbors as "the old lady across the street" and "that couple with the bad kids," maybe it's time to properly introduce yourself. Don't be embarrassed for having taken three years to cross the fence. If "better late than never" wasn't a usable adage, we wouldn't have belated birthday cards.

Just because you don't have an excuse for avoiding the other humans in your immediate habitat doesn't mean its inexcusable—nothing a batch of homemade cookies can't cure. Take your remedy one step further by delivering your tasty tidbits with a copy of Grandma's recipe in hand, typed up on some nice paper or an easy-to-file index card.

Of course, leaving your goodies on the doorstep when your neighbor's at work hardly counts as a step in the right direction. A visit after work may provide the perfect opportunity to make your move without having to stay too long. Use the "Well, smells like you're cooking supper so I'll let you go" excuse if you need a quick getaway.

You may find that your neighbors aren't as bad as you thought. If they invite you in, you may notice that they have the same taste in decorating, have the same books on their shelves, or love "Jeopardy!" as much as you

> "Sometimes I wonder if men and women really suit each other. Perhaps they should live next door and just visit now and then."
> —Katharine Hepburn

do. Either way, take a moment to comment on something that will ease *their* mind that you're not "the psycho single chick next door." (Yes, your neighbors have a label for you, too.)

If the individual approach conjures up images of abduction or hours of tedious chitchat sitting on a couch covered in plastic, take an alternative approach by attending your next tenant picnic, condo association meeting, or block party. You'll get nearly the same effect without the claustrophobia associated with being trapped on a tour of a stranger's home. You can still wow them with your cooking prowess (or deny that the dry brownies are yours), while you move from one introduction to the next in a matter of an hour.

Whatever your decision, you'll be able to rake your front lawn or check your mail without the awkward silence or timid wave that's been holding you hostage for so long. Before you know it, you'll be the most talked about Good Samaritan in Mayberry. Just make sure it's for the right reasons. You may be OK being referred to as "that single chick next door," but who wants to be known as "the girl who steals our paper"?

 Ladies, Start Your Engines!

✳ For some great tips and delicious recipes, visit www.tollhouse.com/index.cfm. Or do your own search with keywords *cookie recipes*.

✳ Shovel snow from an older neighbor's walkway—without asking.

✳ After you get to know her, offer to baby-sit the single mom's kids for a couple hours so she can get some time alone.

✳ Let your neighbors know you're available to pet sit or collect their mail for a weekend if they want to get away.

✳ Share your overabundance of garden vegetables with a neighbor who doesn't have a garden.

22

One Woman's Trash

Spend a day jumping from flea market to thrift store.

When did you last see two men high-fiving after finding a near-new 45 pair of khakis in their size? Or a woman skipping out with an entire dinner set for only five bucks? Secondhand is the way to go if you're looking for a great deal and aren't intent on buying brand new. If you've never tried it, join the ranks of the frugal haut couture. Take a day to dig for treasures in the piles of broken bread boxes and polyester pants and you may find that perfect lamp to fit your eclectic decorating style or perhaps some costume jewelry to complete your uptown look without breaking your downtown bank account.

Need a set of eight dishes for that fancy dinner party you might throw someday? Find a cheap secondhand set. Or better yet, create your own colorful set with a collage of mix-matched pieces. Choose one or two colors and buy a few pieces at a time—a rarer hue will make the hunt even more exciting.

If the idea of real fur makes you sick but you love the look, drop a bill for a faux fur coat or textured suede jacket, courtesy of an ex-hippie's wardrobe overhaul.

For the more crafty, thrift stores and flea markets can offer great rough drafts. From beaten down chairs and night-stands to bland lampshades and plain vases, there's a world of wannabes just waiting for a coat of varnish or a splash of

> "In California, they don't throw their garbage away; they make it into TV shows."
>
> —Woody Allen

paint. And if your supply of supplies is getting low, a thrift store is a great place to stock up on cheap throwaways. Baskets, fabric, paints, wallpaper, and tile can all help turn your humble abode into a princess's palace for a fraction of the cost.

And clothes? Why, the possibilities are endless. Unless you're 7′2″ with a sixteen-inch waist, the racks and stacks will hold at least a few items to fit your style and shape.

Why pay $50.00 for a pair of jeans when you can get them already broken in for $10.00? And sweatshirts for a dollar? You can't beat it. After all, why pay ten bucks for a sweatshirt that you're going to wear only around the house or in your garden? You're not dressing for a business meeting, and you're just going to get it dirty.

Even if the thought of wearing secondhand clothing gives you the willies, you'll be happy to know that many flea markets and some thrift stores now carry new clothes as well. Some are donated from individuals or stores and others are factory seconds or discontinued items. You'll be the first to wear the item, but you'll still get it at a much cheaper price. Now that's a deal even Queen Elizabeth would get excited about.

 Ladies, Start Your Engines!

✳ Check out Goodwill on-line at www.goodwill.org for a peek at what they have to offer.

✳ Don't buy anything that's broken or needs severe mending.

✳ Don't buy anything you "plan" to fit into—unless you're pregnant.

✳ Be sure to try on clothing before you buy it. And don't forget to ask what the store's return policy is. Oftentimes each sale is final or at most you can get only a store credit, so be sure it fits before you take it home.

✳ Wash everything before you wear it.

23

One Hundred Years of Solitude

Interview the town recluse for the local newspaper.

Think you're the only one with an interesting life? Pulleeze! Jump into
your SUV, strap on your seatbelt, and head to the woods to find out
what the town recluse has to say about politics, technology, and fat-
free potato chips. ("Is Jimmy Carter still president?")

You may be surprised to learn that some people actually *survive*
without those things that you take for granted—phones, lights, running water, and even cable. (It's true, some people have never seen
"Sex in the City"!) Although such people may seem unlikely candidates for spilling their guts, you're sure to find a slew of stories just
waiting to hit the front page of the newspaper with your name all over
them. (Ah, the joys of seeing your name in print without a summons
for appearance next to it.)

Even if your hermit of choice does use today's amenities, he or she
is sure to have a rare glimpse into several decades of life in your area.
Ask about specific events or tall tales that have plagued the town streets
since you were a child, or request a "yea or nay" on rumors that the
mayor's office has a secret underground tunnel that runs to what used
to be Miss Betsy's House of Hospitality—or as your grandmother puts
it, "the carnal house of eternal sin and
damnation." Get the skinny on the
town's biggest murder or the truth
about why no one will buy Old Mr.
Kindle's house. Be sure to ask for

> *"Only the suppressed word is
> dangerous."*
>
> —**Ludwig Börne**

photographs to add depth to your story and to jog the memory of the old townie, who may have forgotten some of the juicy details.

There's always a chance that your interviewee *is* the story. Try probing for that "As the World Turns" down and dirty by asking the million-dollar question that no right-minded reporter has done before: "So, why do you hole yourself up in this cave?" The question may sound intrusive, even obnoxious, but when you think about it, what better way to get a hot cover story for the local rag? Do you think Barbara Walters avoids the tough questions with the world's top leaders? Of course not! No one cares why Clinton named his cat "Socks." They want to know if Monica Lewinsky gave good . . . uh . . . birthday presents. The point is, you won't know till you ask the Big One. The worst that can happen is that they'll tell you it's none of your business.

And the *best*-case scenario? You win a Pulitzer prize uncovering the story of the year: "Elvis is alive and living in a tree house in the woods near our town!"

 Ladies, Start Your Engines!

Having trouble getting started? Brush up on tips and tricks with these books:

* *Using Memoirs to Write Local History* (Technical Leaflet 145)

* *How to Interview a Sleeping Man* by Milli Brown

* *The Tape-Recorded Interview: A Manual for Fieldwork in Folklore and Oral History* by Edward D. Ives

24

My Kingdom for a Horse

Saddle up for a day of horseback riding and a night with a sore butt!

If the extent of your bareback riding includes ceramic horses and carnival music, maybe it's time you tried the real McCoy. Transform yourself into the female Lone Ranger with just a few horseback riding lessons. The stable will supply the horse, saddle, and trainer, but you'll be responsible for your own Preparation H. Yeah, riding a horse can be a literal pain in the ass, but imagine the feeling of the wind through your hair (like your hair dryer, but with the smell of moose instead of mousse).

After you take a few lessons and can master the Old Gray Mare's temper, you may find that just the idea of riding a horse makes you feel romantic, even if you're riding alone. Perhaps it reminds you of that full-busted heroine from the cover of those Harlequin paperbacks, or maybe it's the bond you feel with your own Black Beauty. Or what about slipping into the role of the ultimate feminist pioneer, Annie Oakley, whose horse carried her into the history books as one of the original Wild West man-eaters? It won't be long before you start drafting a copy of "Why Horses Are Better than Men." You'll be addicted to the emotional high—it's like riding a motorcycle with legs, only safer and less expensive.

Of course, parting has its sweet sorrow. A few good rides may unleash the equestrian in you and unless you sell

> "I was on a date recently, and the guy took me horseback riding. That was kind of fun, until we ran out of quarters."
>
> —Susie Loucks

your soul to the devil in exchange for a ranch in Wyoming, you probably won't get to see your new baby as much as you like.

Sure, there's always a chance you'll hate it. Or get thrown. Or bitten. Or get hit by an eighteen-wheeler on your way to the stable, but 100 to 1 (what bookie wouldn't take those odds?) says you're gonna want to go back for more.

And the best part about renting a horse for the day is that, unlike other pets, you don't have to clean up after it. You get the advantage of being able to primp and play with your own My Little Pony, but someone else gets the shit work. Literally.

With the exception of being able to sit down for a week, you've got nothing to lose and everything to gain. Saddle up for a day of play with your four-legged kemosabe—it could be the one time you actually *enjoy* having your feet in stirrups.

 Ladies, Start Your Engines!

✳ Whether you're looking for a day ride or an extended trip, find a guide near you at www.findaguide.com/ride.htm.

✳ Going overseas? Incorporate horseback riding into your adventure! Check out some hip horse-vacation ideas at www.horsevacations.com.

✳ Interested in horseback riding as therapy? Get the details at www.ariga.com or search under *horseback riding therapy*.

25

Thyme and Thyme Again

Plant an indoor herb garden in your kitchen window—just keep it legal.

What's up with the price of spices? For the cost of a minijar of oregano you could hire a personal Italian chef instead of slaving over a watery, tasteless sauce of your own. And what the hell is marjoram? As a general rule, if you can't spell it, you don't need it, right?

Then again, your cooking needs all the help it can get, and spices are a quick means to perking up a jar of spaghetti sauce or a microwave meal. Want to add a little peppermint to your tea or homemade vanilla ice cream? How about some pumpkin spice in your grandmother's famous creamy squash soup? Or perhaps some jalapeños for your kick-ass salsa that leaves everyone breathing fire for the rest of the week? If only there were a cheaper solution.

If you're willing to get your hands dirty, there is. Growing your own herbs and spices is an inexpensive way to add a little umph to your family recipes while brightening up your kitchen. If you're willing to invest in a few seeds, potting soil, and a windowsill planter, you're only a step away from being the holistic, self-sufficient, '90s version of Betty Crocker. And unlike your garden, your kitchen plot will practically grow itself. Granted, you'll have to water it (without drowning it), but your

> "Seems I forgot that weeding and sex use up 45, not 40, calories per time segment. Now you have no excuse not to lose that extra five pounds. Get out there and garden."
>
> —Sally Button White

chances of first-degree vegecide are virtually nill. You will, however, have to learn how to reap what you sow. Some spices may need to be picked, peeled, or cleaned before getting stewed on your stove. Don't expect that you can just dump the entire contents of your clay collection into your bubbling brew. Dirt may add protein, but it detracts from the flavor. For a little insight into how to prepare herbs before you use them, pick up *A Cook's Guide to Growing Herbs, Greens, and Aromatics* by Mildred Owen or *The Country Cupboard: Herbs: Imaginative Tips & Sensible Advice for Cooking, Growing, and Enjoying* by Pat Ross.

If your kitchen faces the street or a nosey neighbor, you may want to put those little popsicle sticks in your spicy smorgasbord, just to reassure any law-abiding snitches that your garden contains only potting soil, and not pot. You don't need a ten-man S.W.A.T. team breaking down your front door at three in the morning only to catch you in a deep drooling slumber.

Better yet, share the benefits of your new horticulture hobby by bringing some samples to your neighbors on the shady side of the street. They may even return the favor by sharing a sumptuous treat baked with the products of your window-box harvest. That Italian chef would never cook for free.

 Ladies, Start Your Engines!

Consider some of these tasty herbs:

✳ Sweet basil: Use in Italian dishes and salads. It's soothing to the stomach.

✳ Caraway: Use in soups, breads, and cheeses. The leaves and roots can be eaten as vegetables. You can also use it to extinguish bad breath and indigestion.

✳ Chamomile: Use this tea for digestion problems or as a sleep aid. The leaves and flowers can be used in a fun home facial or as an antiseptic.

✳ Hyssop: This is used by the Benedictine monks to flavor their liqueurs. Use in stews, salads, and soups. It's good in tea for colds, flu, and sore throats.

✳ Valerian: Have this in capsules, tinctures, or boiled in tea to relieve tension, anxiety, and pain. It's easy to grow—can't you feel your anxiety melting already?

26

Captain Stubing, I Presume

Sign up for a singles cruise and see the world through rosé-colored glasses.

Remember how Julie, Isaac, Doc, and Gopher always seemed so happy? Sure, they were rubbing elbows with the rich and famous, and yes, they probably got drinks on the house (or rather, houseboat), but chances are that their incessant bubbliness was due to the fact that they were getting paid to live a life of luxury.

Schmoozing on the seven seas, party hopping from port to port, and playing matchmaker to a shipful of Hollywood icons, what more could you ask for? Sure, life got lonely at times. Julie probably wasn't allowed to get busy with the guests, and the few crew members that we saw were hardly anything to write home about. But what better way to spend your life than getting paid to travel—even if it is in second class?

A singles cruise is an entertainment smorgasbord for the single chick. Even if your love boat turns out to be a dud boat, you'll be getting your money's worth with unlimited drinks, plenty of sunshine, bottomless buffets, and free shuffleboard (although you may have to wait in line for hours behind blue-haired shuffleboard fanatics who stop only to take a sip of their Metamucil martinis).

Despite a variety of structured activities, you can customize the trip to fit your own likes and dislikes. You can take the active approach and bump butts with strangers on the dance floor, or take the

> "Remember all those people on the *Titanic* who waved off the dessert cart?"
>
> —Erma Bombeck

passive approach and cringe at the sight of cheesy dorks with two left feet in the conga line. Get up early for a promenade deck aerobics class or stay up late and get your own step workout stomping to the music of the sizzlin' salsa band. Still too high-energy? Option three: stay in your room with a stack of magazines and books and chow down on a doggie bag from the buffet dessert table.

Getting cabin fever? Hit dry land at the next port with a big empty bag for goodies and enough traveler's checks to bring home a cornucopia of local flair. You can play the tourist role and take lots of pictures, but when it comes time to grab a bite, ask where the locals eat. You'll probably find more authentic eats, and you'll certainly pay much less for it than you would in the restaurant with the "We speak English" sign in the door.

Just be sure to watch your time. Missing your family back home, rush hour traffic, and that huge pile of paperwork on your desk might not be an issue, but missing your boat is a totally different story. You'll pay an arm and a leg to catch up with it at the next port, and you're sure to get a firm scolding from Captain Stubing.

 Ladies, Start Your Engines!

✳ Looking to set the mood before you launch? Check out *African Queen* on video. The more daring might also rent *Joe Versus the Volcano*.

✳ If you would rather read about cruising, spend a day on the dock with *Princess Charming* by Jane Heller or *Final Cruise #03: Farewell Kiss* by Nicole Davidson.

✳ Take along the perfect journal for your trip! Pick up *The Cruise Diary: A Journal for Travelers by Sea* by Michael Carroll.

✳ Ready to get started? Check out any of these great websites for the singles cruise of your dreams!
  • www.singlescruise.com
  • www.cruising.org
  • www.singles-cruise.com
  • www.singlescruises-tours.com

27

Hook, Line, and Sinker

Rent a boat and enjoy a day of fishing, even if you throw 'em back.

Teach a man to fish and feed him forever. Teach a woman to fish and she'll throw it back and buy fish from the market.

Nowadays, fishing is less about feeding your family and more about getting away for the day. Whether you're casting a fly rod into a raging river or chillin' on a boat watching your line bob, fishing can be a relaxing break from a world obsessed with deadlines and deals.

You don't have to be an athlete to enjoy this sport. In fact, some of the best anglers are merely misplaced couch potatoes—surfing the waves instead of the channels, but couch potatoes all the same.

Think of fishing as a day of lounging around doing nothing with the possibility of having something to brag about when you're done. Why do you think it's a sport dominated by men?

Rent a boat for the day or weekend and "deck" yourself out in your skimpiest bikini or mismatched fisherman gear, depending on exactly what type of "catch" you're hoping to make.

If you're not up for piercing live worms, find out what the bait laws are in the area where you'll be dropping a line. Some local ordinances restrict the use of certain types of plastic bait while others won't let you use worms anyway (and who are you to argue?).

> "What I do is called 'fishing.' If it was easy, we would refer to it as catching and there would be a lot more people doing it."
>
> —Linda Greenlaw,
> *The Hungry Ocean*

You'll need to bring a good rod, sunblock, and lots of munchies. Just what kind of food do you bring on a fishing excursion? If you really want to catch fish, quiet food. Stay away from potato chips, celery, and apples, if not to avoid scaring away the fish, then to keep the other hungry boaters from introducing themselves (you're a long way from shore). If you're concerned about the fleets of flirtatious Ishmael wannabes, lonely and desperate after a six-hour voyage at sea, you yourself might choose to take desperate measures. Bring a sort of homemade flag to offer a warning to suitors of the high seas (or low tide): perhaps a drawing of a penis, circled with a line through it, or a giant sign that reads "Warning: PMS in full effect."

Whether you paddle a canoe out to the middle of the lake or peel out into the bay in a mega–horse power speed boat, you're in for a day of relaxation. And if you are out to catch the big one but keep reeling in the minnows, just remember your mom's words of wisdom about men, "There are plenty of fish in the sea, and most of them are too small to satisfy you."

 Ladies, Start Your Engines!

✳ Be sure to find out the entire cost of your boat rental, including deposit and charges for late returns.

✳ Ask about off-season or off-day rates. Wednesdays are probably cheaper than Saturdays.

✳ Request information about specific fishing rules and laws where you'll be boating, including if you need a special boating license for the recreational vehicle you choose.

28

Does This Red Suit Make My Butt Look Big?

Adopt a family at Christmas and get into the spirit by shopping for their goodies.

The bustling crowds, the Christmas Muzak pumping through the speakers, the endless list of gifts to buy and later wrap—not exactly a shopper's dream. Nevertheless, shopping for holiday gifts is a surefire way to get into the spirit of the season. With the exception of putting up your tree or pulling out your Hanukkah candles, nothing marks the beginning of the hubbub like the day after Thanksgiving. The malls are packed, so-called sales are in full swing, and dieters are up against their toughest competition: the never-ending pile of party invitations.

If your heart is as big as your addiction to shopping, why not combine the two by adopting a less fortunate family for the holidays? Once you know their sex and ages you can stir up a shopping spree that would put Imelda Marcos to shame. From toys, trucks, and tiaras to food and fragrances, nothing will brighten your spirit like sharing your outstanding shopping abilities.

Wanna drive the clerks at customer service crazy? Spend the minimum fifty or a hundred dollars for free wrapping by raking in tons of small-ticket items like sample-size fragrances, tiny teddy bears, slippers, and ornaments—then turn the bag over to the wrapping delegate. Be sure to ask for a random mix of all their paper variety before returning to part two of your shopping bonanza: the holiday hogfest at the food court.

> "Americans are always trying to do the right thing—after they've tried everything else."
> —Winston Churchill

When you return home with your packages, be sure to hide them in a safe place. Pets are sure to develop a sudden plague of curiosity and should be informed of the gifts contents and intended recipients in advance. Although phrases like, "These are not for you" and "You wouldn't like this fragrance anyway" are simple and effective tactics with both dogs and cats, placing your finds in a steel safe buried twenty feet underground can't hurt. If your pet catches you doing so, you can always allay its suspicions of mistrust by explaining that December is the most common month for house fires.

When delivering the gifts to your sponsor family, remember that first impressions are everything. Why not go all out and dress in a Santa suit? Be sure your suit is a vibrant red, not a faded mauve, and that your boots are shined and free of "yard presents" from your pets. (You may want to skip the chimney entrance on account of being inexperienced in the ways of immaculate delivery.) Drop off your gifts with a cheery "ho ho ho" and take comfort in the fact that 1) you've just helped a family enjoy the holidays, 2) you put your talent for shopping to good use and, 3) you didn't eat enough to fill out that red suit.

 Ladies, Start Your Engines!

✳ Contact a local church or other place of worship that can provide you with the name of a family in need.

✳ Be sure to get the age and sex of each child to determine the best items to give.

✳ If you're unsure about which gifts would be appropriate, ask a sales clerk to offer some fun suggestions.

✳ Ask about free gift wrap. If you're under the necessary spendature for free wrapping, tell the clerk at the store or mall that these are gifts for needy families. He or she may be willing to cut you a break.

29

Slinging Hash for Those Less Fortunate

Volunteer at a soup kitchen to feed your spiritual hunger.

Perhaps you have an internal yearning to change the world or a need to become more involved in your community and its outreach programs. Or maybe there's just nothing on TV. Whatever your reasoning, no one's going to complain if you help feed the homeless at your local shelter. Whether you live in a small town or a booming metropolis, chances are your nearest food bank is understaffed and in need of volunteers. Sure, handing out food isn't as glamorous as having your picture in the paper as chairwoman of the United Way Ball, and it may not be as upbeat as a rock 'n' roll benefit concert, but feeding hungry people is about as useful as you can get when it comes to non-profit work. You don't need any specialized skills (so you can stop worrying that your spaghetti sauce will be too bland), and you don't have to sell yourself to the head of any committee ("and when I was twelve, I was nominated by my classmates as most likely to try to give a homeless man a makeover").

Of course, feeding homeless and low-income families does have its disadvantages. You'll be face to face with poverty, which can lead you down one of three paths. You may leave feeling the need to 1) watch seven straight hours of "Joanie Loves Chachi" to clear your mind, 2) track down your mayor on the golf course to ask him what he's doing about the number of families below

"Let them eat cake."
—Marie Antoinette

the poverty line, or 3) donate your Chocolate of the Month membership to the shelter.

The good news is you'll never get laid off from your volunteer work. All those gifts that you think go underappreciated at your current place of employment will earn you top billing on the server roster. A smiling face is as valuable as a gourmet chef or top-notch electrician when you're standing behind the counter serving up meat and potatoes. If you don't believe it, think of the last time you had really horrible food but really friendly service. You still left your waitperson a good tip, didn't you? (If you didn't, you should be ashamed. She doesn't cook your food, she carries it to the table! Would you refuse to pay your baby-sitter if your kids trashed the house?)

The point is, just being your usual perky self (and lifting a ladle) is enough. So if you're looking for an excuse, don't bother—unless you don't have enough money to put gas in your car and you can't afford the bus to get to the shelter, in which case, keep the Chocolate of the Month membership. You could use the endorphin rush.

 ## Ladies, Start Your Engines!

✳ Call the shelter directly and ask them if they need help. Get a list of preferred times and dates for you to serve meals or help cook.

✳ Don't be afraid to ask for a specific duty. If you want only to help serve (and you refuse to do dishes), let the director know up front to avoid an embarrassing situation later.

✳ Call churches and homeless shelters to find out if they run soup kitchens. Most churches will not require that you be a member to volunteer.

✳ Don't wear your best clothes or your worst. Try something in between that doesn't need to be dry cleaned if food splatters on it.

30

Oh, Solo Mia!

Join the Culture Club with a night at the opera, symphony, or ballet.

Now that you're all grown up, you should know that today's theater
experience entails much more than two hours of nonstop making out
and groping in the balcony. From the tear-jerking tragedies of *Rigiletto*
to the spirit-lifting sashays of *Swan Lake*, today's fine-art events offer
something for every mood, interest, and attention span.

If you've never been to a so-called cultured event, get around the
novice nervousness with any of these eight simple suggestions:

1. Ask friends or relatives to fill you in on some of their favorites,
    then check the local paper for events you can afford.

2. Many of the more famous creations have been put on video.
    Rent a few or just check out the back of the box to get an idea
    of what you'll be watching—especially if it's in another lan-
    guage.

3. Call ahead to find out what is considered appropriate attire.
    Smaller, lesser-known shows may suggest work attire, while
    more formal and famous events, like the Boston Symphony
    Orchestra's sold-out fund-raiser, may require formal evening
    wear. (You'll finally get to wear those pearls you got for
    graduation!)

4. Stop by the theater and pick up
    some brochures to browse the list
    of upcoming events or call and ask

> **"The opera isn't over till the fat
> lady sings."**
>
> -Dan Cook

to be placed on the theater's mailing list. Your mail carrier will be impressed.

5. Check the Web for synopses of events coming to your town.

6. Buy a few tapes or CDs to brush up on your classical music. If your head starts bobbing by the middle of it, you may want to try an opera or ballet—they tend to be more visually stimulating.

7. Read reviews in your local paper or arts and entertainment weekly.

8. Call the theater's hot line and listen to their descriptions of the performances.

If you're still not sure, take a chance and buy a ticket to an event that won't break your bank. If worst comes to worst, think of it as an excuse to dress up for a date that won't involve small talk, back hair, or bad breath. You can leave your polite date laugh at home, but be sure to bring your opera glasses. If nothing else, you can drool over Baryshnikov's butt in tights.

 Ladies, Start Your Engines!

✳ Eat before you go. Even a candy wrapper is enough to crack the silence of a huge theater.

✳ If you're a habitual gum popper (yeah, you know who you are), leave the gum at home to avoid a potentially embarrassing situation.

✳ Watch for supertitles, the English translation of the words to the songs in an opera. They are usually projected on a large screen above the stage so you have a better understanding of what's going on.

31

Party of One

Get decked out and head to an upscale restaurant for a gourmet meal over a trashy novel.

"Is someone joining you?" "How many in your party?" (Certainly not just one!) "Would you like to wait in the lounge until the rest of your group arrives?" If you've never heard any of these phrases, then you've probably never gone out to eat alone. There's a societal assumption that a woman entering a restaurant alone is either looking for some-one who's already seated or waiting for the other half of her party to arrive. Why is this? Certainly, throughout the course of time at least one woman has had the pleasure of eating out alone—be it an upscale restaurant or a downtown diner—other than a food critic.

The key to eating alone, and getting the respect you deserve while doing so, is to come prepared. Mace is good for walking to your car after dark, and a good trashy novel is a relaxing way to unwind while you're waiting for your meal. Do not, however, feel you have to bring reading material. If you'd rather stare out the window or let your eyes wander around the restaurant, feel free to do so. No one says you have to be busy. If you do choose to bring something to read, why not make it worth your while? Choose titles that are sure to keep away unwanted prey, like, *How to Kill a Man in His Sleep* or *So You Wanna Be a Nun*.

The good news about dining alone is that you can spend as much or as little as you want. Long gone are the days of pressure to put out for your rabid consumption of a thirty-dollar lobster special. You can eat like

> "Her face was her chaperone."
> —Rupert Hughes

a slob if you want, pick up food with your fingers, or smile at the prospect of cradling a huge piece of spinach between your front teeth. And, as long as you have a safe ride home, drink up! The only person that'll be taking advantage of your wine sampling is the waiter, who will probably look for a hefty tip after making so much dinner conversation with "the lonely single lady at table four." (Watch for random peeks from the kitchen staff.)

So as you venture out into the world of single-chick chow-down, remember the golden rules of preparedness. And if the hostess greets you with the predictable assumption, respond with the always tactful, "The only person I'm waiting for will be bringing my menu."

 ### Ladies, Start Your Engines!

✳ Call ahead to make a reservation for one person. It may help ease tension upon your arrival.

✳ Ask the hostess for a private booth or a table by the window to avoid getting plopped at a table in the center of the restaurant.

✳ If you would prefer, ask if they serve dinner at the tables in the bar. You can catch up on the news or the big game or chat up the hunky bartender.

32

Shaken, Not Stirred

Stop into a posh jazz club for cocktails and cool tunes.

The nightclub scene seems to offer rather dismal options, don't you think? If you hang out at a college watering hole where frat boys try to mooch beer money off you, there's a 50/50 chance you'll get barfed on. Hit a dance club, and the hyper flashing lights and accompanying techno tunes will make your head throb, and anyway, everyone there is hotter than you and has the vinyl hotpants to prove it.

Break out of bar scene banality by hitting a jazz club! If you think jazz music sounds too snooty, or you associate it with Kenny G elevator schlock, don't knock it before you try it. Real jazz is not the stuff you hear when the gas company puts you on hold. "Real" jazz can be many things, including the freeform funkiness of bebop, big swing bands, the Dixieland stuff your dad likes, or pulsing latin-flavored fun. And jazz is one of the few musical art forms that originated here in the good ol' U.S. of A. So consider it your patriotic duty to expand your musical horizons! You're sure to have a blast while you're at it.

Not into music, you say? A jazz bar is a worthwhile diversion for the ambiance alone, especially with upscale nightclubs. You'll notice a distinct lack of tacky decor found in other bars (we challenge you to find a single neon Budweiser sign or Coors Light bikini babe poster!). Your drink will be served in an actual glass, rather than a plastic keg cup. Not only that, at last you'll be able to sit at your table and enjoy

> "If you have to ask what jazz is, you'll never know."
>
> —Louis Armstrong

yourself without an errant stage diver or mosh pit participant slamming into you.

Not only is the crowd bound to be more sophisticated, the drinks might be, too! Forget ordering a drink from some barkeep who's too busy adjusting his nose ring and eyeballing the chicks on the dance floor to master bartenderdom beyond pouring a draft beer (and if it's a Guinness, even that can be too much!). Chances are, order a decent drink in a jazz bar, and they will actually be able to make it for you, even if it's a Shirley Temple on the rocks. This is the one place where you can dress like Audrey Hepburn, perch on a barstool while flaunting a long cigarette holder, and still fit in!

But the best part of hanging out at a jazz club is the views! Unlike the hayseeds you'd meet at a country bar or the frosty-haired club kids at the dance scene, jazz clubs seem to attract the brainy-yet-cool types. Something about quality music attracts those tousled, bespectacled types that slouch in the corner wearing their cool suits with that "Oh, am I hot?" aloofness. So slam down that vodka martini, launch into a conversation about funk vs. freeform, and ask if the two of you might bebop the night away!

 Ladies, Start Your Engines!

* Check to see if there's a national act playing at your club of choice before you show up—for the most popular shows, you might have to buy a ticket ahead of time.

* Consider going on a weeknight rather than Friday or Saturday. The cover's usually cheaper, and there's more room to mingle or find a table.

* If you like a certain band, ask if they've got a CD out. Lots of bands sell their CDs at their shows.

33

Vote "No" on Amendment 2 to Ban Rallies!

Organize a rally for (or against) something that needs changing.

How many times have you read or heard about an injustice in society but done nothing about it? For most, the number is somewhere around ∞. From animal abuse and pesticides to the Ku Klux Klan and nuclear power plants, atrocities are all around us. But what can one person do to make a difference? Organize a rally!

If you really want to change things, the best way to shake 'em up is to call attention to the issue. Oftentimes the only reason that bad things go unchanged is that no one knows there's a problem. Organizing a picket line, a lock-in, or a prayer gathering can garner your cause the attention it needs. While there's always a chance you'll be hauled away in a paddy wagon, wouldn't you be willing to spend a night in the slammer to protect an innocent seal from being clubbed, a fox from being trapped, or an elephant from being chased down for its ivory?

This is not to say that you should chain yourself to the Dutch elm disease–infected tree in your park to prevent it from being cut down. It's also not recommended that you go *looking* for a cause in order to cut in line on the escalator going up to the Pearly Gates. Standing up for something you believe in, however, is certainly a noble act, and sometimes it requires you to go beyond letter writing and community petitions.

> "Those are my principles. If you don't like them, I have others."
> —Groucho Marx

Say, for example, that a developer wants to cut down your nearby forest to build a supermall. Where will all the animals go? Unless the squirrels have suddenly figured out a way to pass their driver's exam, they aren't renting a U-Haul to transport the forest's inhabitants to a new locale.

And what about that article you read that said the Humane Society is being forced to close due to lack of funding? Staging a rally may be just what the nonprofit organization needs to raise enough money (and awareness) to keep its doors open for homeless pups and felines.

Whatever cause you choose to support or protest, make sure your intentions are honest. If that mom-and-pop coffee shop is being run off the block by the big conglomerates and you can't bear to see it go, make sure it's because the owners have been a pillar of the community for years, and not because you still haven't gotten the phone number of that hottie behind the counter.

 ### Ladies, Start Your Engines!

✳ Find out what's legal before you plan your rally. You may want to stash away a little bail money—just in case.

✳ Make sure your cause is a deserving one. No sense getting harassed—or arrested— just for trying to keep your boss from removing the vending machine in the snack room.

✳ Tell a friend where you're going so that if you don't call her by a certain time, she can let your dog out. It could be a long night.

34

Self-Steam Your Windows

Park at Inspiration Point and contemplate the city lights. You'll be the only one not arrested for public nudity.

Think the idea of "parking" is reserved for your parents' generation? Maybe at one time, but much like Dick Clark, the icons of the 1950s keep resurfacing. (Really, did making out ever go out of style?)

The good news is, parking at your favorite remote nightspot is a form of free entertainment. You've got a view of the city lights, the peace and quiet of nature, and the R-rated version of "Happy Days" in the car next door. Sure, you could get some accusations of being a pervert, but chances are your late-night porn stars are going to be too busy sucking face to notice you enjoying your front-row seat with an oversize bag of homemade popcorn. Depending on the climate and just how hot and bothered your auto neighbors get, you may not have much of a view due to the steam. But look on the bright side, you can always steam your own windows to ward off would-be perverts.

Why not bring a sultry tape to soothe your savage day at work? A collection of Barry White's greatest hits or Harry Connick Jr.'s latest will do the trick. You can melt away your troubles and take a stroll down memory lane with that sexy ex that keeps popping up in your dreams or that cutie at the video store check-out.

If you're not worried about your battery dying, bring the latest X-rated bestseller and indulge yourself in a little

> "I'm going to the backseat of my car with the woman I love, and I won't be back for *ten minutes.*"
>
> —Homer Simpson

fictitious fantasy via Jackie Collins. If you can't conjure up a dream date, let someone create one for you.

One word of caution: Be sure to keep your doors locked. The last thing you need is to get carjacked by the Inspiration Point Stalker or worse—to have a horny teenager climb into the wrong car by accident. Under the cover of night he might mistake you for his ripe and ready cheerleader girlfriend who snuck her parents' car out of the garage to consummate their torrid matching-tattoo love affair.

On the other hand, you could put on your best "Kiki" voice and make the best of it. You'd probably be the first person to pick someone up at Inspiration Point. Then again, if he's still in high school, the cop knocking on your window is going to give you more than a warning.

Hmmm. A man in uniform. Now that's something to get your windows steamed.

 Ladies, Start Your Engines!

✳ Be sure you know the area before you head out after dark to find the perfect spot.

✳ Make sure you have plenty of gas. You don't want your tank getting low when you're in the middle of nowhere.

✳ Don't run your battery for too long. The last thing you want is to have to knock on some steamy windows to ask for a jump start.

35

My Husband Left Me for Another Woman—Let's Celebrate!

Take a line-dancing lesson and bring your hanky for the honky-tonk music.

Country music is living proof that misery loves company. Where else can you hear a good ol' boy wailing about the sadness of losing his woman, his dog, and his house—besides in a cell block in Arkansas? Apparently someone is taking comfort in his loss. After all, country music is hotter than ever, with sales figures that'll turn an unemployed whiner into an upscale playboy faster than you can say, "All my exes live in Texas."

Why not jump on the bandwagon and boogie down with the toe-tappin' twosomes like the saucy swinging single that you are? You don't need a partner to sign up for country line dancing. It's really the perfect scenario. By the time you are ready to hit the Saturday night scene, you'll be in your shining hour (having trained your two left feet in the presence of strangers on a few Tuesday nights). You'll look like a natural, despite your love affair with big-city life, and no one will be the wiser to your former life of hip hop and rock 'n' roll.

Even the most basic classes will teach you how to combine your stomps, wings, and steps to master more than one dance, as the majority of moves are generally just rearranged to fit each song.

If you really want to look the part, break out your jeans, cowboy boots and hat, and button-down shirt, complete with at least enough hanging

> "I worry that the person who thought up Muzak may be thinking up something else."
>
> —Lily Tomlin

tassels to blow your nose on when you hear the lyrics to the honky-tonk tunes that provide your backbeat. The crooning cowboys may leave you feeling sorry for them, but it'll lift your spirits knowing that someone else has it worse than you. In fact, you may just want to kick up your heels as an expression of joy at just how good your life is: You've got a good job, great friends, enough cash to afford the luxury of learning a few new dance moves, and most important, you don't have to dress like this every day. (Tassels really should be reserved for graduation caps, curtain tiebacks, and strippers with superhuman talent, don't you think?)

 ### Ladies, Start Your Engines!

* Check your phone book for dance studios that offer country line dancing. If they don't, ask if they know of ones that do.

* Call your closest country-western bar or club. Many offer classes on off-nights or during the day on weekends.

* Ask a friend who knows how to dance to teach you a few moves or to recommend a good instructor.

* Check a video store or on-line for lessons on videotape so you can learn in the privacy of your own home. Try *Line Dancing the Country Way Vol. 1* or *Country Dancing Made Easy*.

* Wanna practice at home first or get into the spirit of things during your commute to work? Pick up *Christy Lane's Line Dancing Music* on CD or cassette.

36

What Color Is Your Parachute?

Jump feet first into your fear as you tandem skydive 14,000 feet over the earth.

So maybe this isn't one of those times someone can say to you, "What's the worst that can happen?" Even if you've never tried jumping out of a plane, you've probably dropped an egg at some point in your life and therefore can come to your own conclusions about the worst-case scenario.

Statistically, your chances of getting hurt are very slim, as it's really more of an all-or-nothing situation. So perk up! Skydiving is actually a very safe sport. You'll be properly trained and, depending on just how many classes you plan to take, you can jump alone or with the safety of an experienced flight instructor strapped to your chest. (OK, you're actually piggybacked onto the instructor, but the other way makes you sound more in control.)

If you excel to the point of jumping alone, you'll enjoy the same views and flying sensations but with a slightly greater feeling of responsibility (i.e., you'll be pulling the parachute cord yourself). If you're the nervous type and think there's a chance that if your main chute doesn't open you'll pass out—rendering you unable to pull your reserve cord—stick to the piggyback jump. Your instructor will have jumped enough to know she's not going to freak at the first sign of trouble, and you can lean back and enjoy the ride without the pressure of thinking.

> **"I'm desperately trying to figure out why kamikaze pilots wore helmets."**
>
> —Dave Edison

If you know people who have jumped before, ask them about their experience and why they enjoyed it (or didn't). Chances are they'd do it again if they had the time and financial resources. You'd be hard-pressed to find someone who hated skydiving—unless they have a horror story to share.

Not in it for the long haul? Sign up for the piggyback jump. You won't need a series of classes, just one day of preliminary explanations of precautionary measures. It's the fastest way to actually get in a plane—and get out of one. Take heed, though, you may find yourself itching for a second jump. With an endorphin rush and view unparalleled by any other sport (and a natural windblown 'do unrivaled by even Hollywood's top hairdressers), jumping out of a plane at 40,000 feet may become less of a one-time fling (pardon the pun) and more of a monthly "must do." Or would that be "mussed 'do"?

 Ladies, Start Your Engines!

✳ Call some of the small airports nearby to ask if they offer skydiving lessons or tandem jumps.

✳ Don't forget to ask about costs, experience of your instructor, licenses, and what to wear for your jump.

✳ Ask about money-back policies if you cancel, whether due to scheduling problems or chickening out at the last minute.

✳ Check with your insurance company. Not to scare you, but some policies don't cover skydiving in the event of your death or even if you become injured. Ask the skydiving company if you're covered under its insurance policy during a tandem jump.

37

Waiting to Exhale

Take a day to deep-sea dive or just practice in a scuba shop's oversize tank.

What if Don Ho's reference to "Tiny Bubbles" was actually about scuba diving? How drastically would that change your image of the famous song? Would visions of flippers, scuba tanks, and full wet suits dance in your head?

If you've never taken the deep-sea plunge, consider taking a mini-vacation to discover what the world of underwater adventure has to offer. You don't necessarily have to splurge on two weeks in the Caribbean just to learn the ways of the waves. Many larger cities in the United States now offer indoor scuba tanks to give you the feel of swimming in full gear, teach you how to work your equipment, and get you used to the idea of breathing through a giant bendy straw. Call around to find out how much one or two lessons will cost before emptying your savings account on an all-you-can-swim vacation in a more remote locale.

Although a practice session at your local tank or pool won't offer much of a view or interaction with live creatures, other than your stealthy seal (ex–Navy S.E.A.L., that is), you'll get comfortable with your equipment and be able to gracefully maneuver around in full-body pantyhose. Sure, it takes some getting used to, but you'll love the way a wet suit nips and tucks for a fraction

> "If I walked on water, people would say I couldn't swim."
> —John Turner

of the cost of plastic surgery. ("What *is* that miracle material, and where can I buy it—by the truckload?")

If and when you are ready to hit the deep sea, look for vacation packages that include the price of scuba diving. Many of the larger resorts and cruises offer it in the price of the complete package. Don't get caught paying extra for the one thing you want to do most on your "all-inclusive" vacation getaway.

Even if you opt for a one-day session off the coast, be sure to bring the essentials: waterproof sunblock and a waterproof camera. If you don't have a camera that takes pics underwater (and who does have one of those just lying around the house?), ask the instructor if the company offers loaners so you can take a few shots for your scrapbook. When else will you see purple and violet fish outside of the mall pet store? And even Trixie's Tropical Pets can't offer a close encounter with a Monroe.

Whether your goal is to practice close to home or to take a luxury lesson off shore, be prepared to marvel at the wonders of ocean life. You may think you're living the good life now, but when you slide into a new dimension and come face-to-face with creatures you've seen only in *National Geographic* and *Omni*, the best advice you can heed is "Don't look a seahorse in the mouth."

 Ladies, Start Your Engines!

✳ Leave your jewelry on the beach. Some creatures, such as electric eels, are attracted to shiny metals.

✳ Don't ever dive alone, not even right off the coast. Riptides can catch you in as little as two feet of water and drag you under or out to sea.

✳ Everything you wanted to know about diving but were afraid to ask can be found at Scuba Chat: www.scubachat.com.

✳ Find a dive center near you at: www.divedirectory.com.

38

Can I Have S'more Bug Spray?

Pitch a tent at a campground or in your backyard and rough it for a night.

Think you're becoming a bit too much of a pampered princess in your penthouse in the sky? Try trading in your silk pajamas for a night of flannel shirts and knee-high waders.

With the sky for your ceiling, the stars for your night light, and Mother Earth as your mattress, you'll learn why roughing it is a great way to build your self-confidence while putting a little hair on your chest (and your legs). Even if you pitch a tent in your own backyard, you're bound to get spooked by something: a screeching owl, the howling wind, or even an accidental glimpse of your neighbor skinny-dipping at midnight. No matter, though. The experience will be one more to add to your list of Brave Things That Sucked at the Time but Seem Really Cool Now.

Of course, camping will do more than boost your self-esteem. You may actually have fun! Be sure to pack the essentials for an entire day and night of solo sleepover superfun. Here are a few "must-haves" for your overnight adventure:

* That huge stack of magazines that are so outdated your living room could double for a dentist's waiting area
* Chocolate bars, marshmallows, and graham crackers to make s'mores, even if you have to eat them cold (thanks to some stupid

> "If a man speaks in the forest and no woman is there to hear him, is he still wrong?"
> —Anonymous

tenant law about not building a bonfire in the backyard—bah humbug!)

* Flashlight, portable radio or headset, lots of batteries, and a huge collection of chick music (leave the horror Books on Tape at home)

* A cooler with lots of ice and drinks and a knapsack full of miscellaneous snacks (Don't forget the can opener if you want to take advantage of your time alone by eating a can of baked beans.)

* Bug spray, sunscreen, a folding chair, a crossword puzzle book, some stationery, a notebook or journal, sunglasses, a hat, and a pocketknife (complete with toenail clippers, melon baller, and tweezers for random splinters or stray eyebrow hairs)

* Swimsuit and fishing pole if you're leaving the comfort of your backyard or have moved your aquarium outside for the day

If you've got a canine camping companion, be sure to bring a leash and rope in case Rover tries to wander. Your barking buddy may be enough to ease your mind under the cover of darkness, but you don't want him getting a wild hair (or a wild hare!) especially when you're trying to chow down on your sixth s'more. Not that anyone's counting.

 Ladies, Start Your Engines!

* Set up your tent in a flat spot, but not a low point. If it rains, you could end up sleeping in a pool.

* Put your sleeping bag on a pad or air mattress to keep you warm, comfortable, and dry if the tent leaks.

* Learn how to put your rain fly on *before* it rains. You don't have to keep it on if it's sunny out (keeping it off will help ventilate the tent), but you don't want to be reading directions in the middle of a rain storm.

39

An Apple a Day

**Spend the day at an orchard and get your RDA
of fruits and veggies.**

If you love the smell of hot apple pie, you'll really love the scent of fresh apples baking in the mid-afternoon sun. Orchards, much like sperm banks, are a great place to choose your own goods without a middle man. Unlike a sperm bank, however, you don't have to pay for damaged goods. Find a bruised apple? Just leave it on the tree for the next less-studious apple picker.

Thanks to the marvels of modern technology, pesticides, and the pollution-birthed hole in the ozone layer, many of today's orchards are able to grow fruits and vegetables outside their "should-be" climate zones. Consider it one-stop shopping for the fruit enthusiast or vegan-child trying to break free of the usual peanut butter cup regimen.

If you're planning to make a day of it, strap on a book bag to hold your day's catch. Don't worry about using one of those little green quart containers the orchard supplies. Most orchards charge by the weight, not the container. Just be sure to take the books out of your backpack, or you'll be paying Russian toilet paper prices for your produce.

What better way to complete your day than by incorporating your Pilgrim-like harvesting skills into your own fall feast? Warm the house with the smell of fresh raspberry muffins or apple strudel, or stock up on homemade orange marmalade and blackberry preserves. Put that dusty juice maker to use with a miraculous fruit smoothie, or just sit on your

> "One that would have the fruit
> must climb the tree."
> —**Thomas Fuller**

front porch competing in the first annual Watermelon Seed–Spitting Olympics.

Were your eyes bigger than your stomach on your four-hour plucking excursion? Put your surplus to good use by creating fruit baskets for your neighbors, friends, or family. Just wrap a mixture of your leftovers in colored cellophane and tie with a ribbon or secure with a rubber band and bow. No one can resist such a healthy and fresh gift, especially knowing you've picked the fruit with your own two hands. (No one has to know you had fun doing it!)

Of course, spending a day at the orchard is about much more than picking fruit. You'll probably get some exercise, sample some real cider, and perhaps even catch a hayride. Hey! Maybe you're not such a city girl after all.

Then again, you did try to tip the tractor driver.

 Ladies, Start Your Engines!

✳ Dress in layers. A cool morning can easily turn into a hot summer afternoon out in the field. Also, leave your good clothes and shoes at home. Berry juice stains, and horses tend to "go where they stand."

✳ Bring gloves. Depending on how long you plan to pick, your hands may get chafed, blistered, or cut by branches.

✳ Call first. Some orchards are open for only a few months out of the year or may run out of crops earlier than a brochure indicates. Call ahead to avoid a wasted trip.

40

Sold! To the Woman Who Loves Junk

Attend an antique auction for some steals and deals, and search for a Picasso among the junk.

If you thought you talked fast as a teenager, imagine being the parent of an auctioneer: "ThenIwaslikeOhmyGod!Hesaidthattoyou?What-didyoudo?Iwouldhavedied!He'ssocute!IsitnexttohiminalgebraandI'm-alwayslikeOhmyGodyou'resocute!"

Today's auctioneers have good reason to talk fast. They've got to move a lot of junk and move it quickly. Perhaps the theory is that by talking too rapidly to be understood by the human brain, the auction-eer will get you to bid on items before you have time to realize just how ugly, useless, and overpriced they really are. Of course, there are always exceptions to the rule, and if you know how to distinguish the trash from the treasure *before* you bid, you're likely to walk away with a great find.

Look for an auction with lots to choose from and arrive early enough to wade through the offerings before the bidding begins. Take a notepad and pen and jot down the items that most appeal to you along with what you're willing to spend to make them yours. This will keep you from overbidding when the Fastest Mouth in the South starts his spiel. A preliminary viewing will also give you a close-up inspection of the mer-chandise up for bid. Are there cracks and chips that might otherwise go unnoticed from your seat six rows back? Does that broken cabinet merely need a new hinge

81

"If women didn't exist, all the money in the world would have no meaning."

—Aristotle

or an entire new door? Is that antique vase from the seventeenth century or the Seventeenth Street dollar store?

If you want to be really prepared, bring a book to look up the value of antiques and collectibles. Several good ones are on the market and if you're interested in a particular niche (e.g., porcelain dolls, old tins, or antique toys) you can focus your efforts on that category. But no, there's not a book for evaluating old makeup. Throw it out. That color will never be back in style, and that mascara from 1982 is likely to cake your eyes closed for good.

Nervous about accidentally bidding on something you can't afford by rubbing your nose or scratching your dandruff? Don't be. With the exception of the snooty, big-wig bid-offs, most of today's auctions use paddles or an old-fashioned raise of the hand. If you're still concerned, bring your own makeshift paddle to keep your intentions clear, or sit on your hands until that newly discovered Picasso finds a home.

 Ladies, Start Your Engines!

✳ Try to pay by credit card so that if you don't get the merchandise, you can challenge the charges with your credit card issuer.

✳ Ask about return policies and how and where you can get service on your items if you need it—for electronics, for example.

✳ Read reviews about the seller and avoid buying from those with negative comments.

✳ Pick up a copy of *Auction This!: Your Complete Guide to the World of Online Auctions* by Dennis L. Prince.

✳ Brush up on some of the top on-line auctions:
  • www.ebay.com
  • www.ubid.com
  • www.buybidwin.com

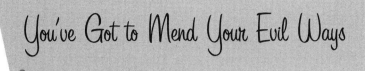

41

You've Got to Mend Your Evil Ways

Expand your wardrobe with a sewing class for even the most needlephobic.

How many times have you uttered the phrase "I have nothing to wear"? Unless you're a nudist, that's probably an extreme exaggeration, but as a woman, you are legally entitled to complain about your wardrobe's lack of diversity four times per year (once per season, according to the National Society for Attire Complaints). The exceptions to that rule are those who know how to sew. Professional and amateur seamstresses alike are limited to one complaint per year due to their own self-determined skills. (Think of it in terms of a Ben and Jerry's employee complaining he has nothing to eat.)

So (or rather, "sew"), if you're ready to take up the challenge of learning to knit, crochet, stitch, or macrame, you'll soon be looking at a bottomless pit of fashion (a lot like the wardrobe in C. S. Lewis's *The Lion, the Witch, and the Wardrobe*). Your clothes will fit like a glove thanks to the tailor who knows you best, and the options for color, fabric, and pattern are limited only by your imagination—and, of course, what's on sale at Felicia's Fabric Barn.

First, check with your local fabric stores. Many offer free or inexpensive sewing classes on the assumption that you'll buy your supplies through them. Then, consider what your main interests are. If you're looking to create matching curtains for your bedroom or a giant pillow for Queen Kitty's sleeping pleasure,

> "I base most of my fashion taste on what doesn't itch."
>
> **—Anonymous**

Intro to Sewing might be the class for you. If, on the other hand, you're hoping to crochet a sweater to get back at Aunt Martha for all those winters you were off balance due to sleeves of different lengths, opt for Beginner's Knitting. If you've retained the basics from eighth grade home ec and you feel you're ready to move on to the big leagues, ask about intermediate classes. You might decide to create your own line of creative couture, generating some interest (and maybe a little pocket change) from your friends with good taste.

If nothing else, you'll learn how to stitch up a few things for around your house: the comforter Queen Kitty just *had* to knead, the lucky socks that won you those free concert tickets, and the size-10 khakis you loaned to your best friend who tried to stuff her size-14 ass into them.

 Ladies, Start Your Engines!

✳ *No Time to Sew: Fast & Fabulous Patterns & Techniques for Sewing a Figure-Flattering Wardrobe* by Sandra Betzina will provide you with some great tricks of the trade.

✳ Visit an on-line sewing community at www.sewing.com.

✳ Learn to sew by video! Pick up *You Can Make It—Learn to Sew, Level 1*. Director: Michael Tripaldi Jr.

42

Dancing in the Streets

Host a block party and become the most talked about chick in the neighborhood.

Wanna get your neighbors in an uproar? Throw a block party to challenge the party poopers and couch potatoes to make some resolutions that entail more than "Friends" reruns and nay-saying normality.

Check the forecast in the *Farmer's Almanac* and aim for a weekend predicting warm weather (you don't want all those freaks in your house, do you?). Draw up eye-catching posters and personally pass them out to neighbors to cut down your chances of offending anyone who insists on a personal invitation. Hang up some posters on telephone poles around your block and be sure to indicate the time you're planning to get things rolling. You don't want to be woken up by the early birds on your one day to sleep in. (Yes, there are people who drink in the morning. Whadaya think mimosas are for?)

If you have a lot of kids in your neighborhood and don't want to be responsible for them sneaking drinks from your set-up, you may want to implement a BYOB plan, or if you're feeling charitable and want to earn some brownie points with those hotties across the street, hook up a keg in your front yard. Just be sure you've got a trustworthy bartender who will check IDs. You don't want to be hauled away from your own soiree!

You may want to call your district adviser to ask about the area's road block policy. It's not pretty when a bunch of drunks start jumping out in front

> "Live so that you wouldn't be ashamed to sell the family parrot to the town gossip."
>
> —Will Rogers

of oncoming cars. Nothing kills a good buzz like the need for an ambulance.

Even a dry party can be a good party. If you have a neighbor who's in a band, ask him if he would consider setting up for the day to earn some word-of-mouth references. Ditto with clowns, mimes, gymnasts, skateboarders, or magicians, who might work for tips if they think you can draw a big enough crowd.

Consider renting a few tables and set up a potluck buffet, indicating on your posters that each household should bring at least one dish or nonalcoholic beverage. And keep a few garbage cans around the area to avoid leaving your block looking like New York City after a ticker tape parade. Your reputation for hosting the year's greatest party can turn on you in less than twenty-four hours if the morning after the neighbors find stray dogs chowing down on litter.

 Ladies, Start Your Engines!

✳ Not sure about the rules and regulations? Avoid spending a night in jail by reviewing some of the general guidelines and laws before you get your party started.

✳ Circulate a sign-up sheet a week before the block party to ensure you'll get help with set-up and tear-down of tables, chairs, posters, and sound systems.

✳ Make each neighbor responsible for decorating his or her own house and yard. Be sure to solicit help for elderly neighbors.

43

The Apple Doesn't Fall Far from the Tree

Trace your lineage and map out your family tree—you'll finally understand where all the nuts come from!

You know that reserve bottle of mind-numbing, 100-proof scotch that you've been saving just in case Grandma starts to tell her Growing Up in Ireland story for the 612th time? The story that, without fail, sends your eyeballs rolling to the back of your head? "There was nothing but potatoes. Potatoes for breakfast. Potatoes for lunch. We had to walk to school uphill in the snow, both directions, in clogs carved out of potatoes. . . ." Well, dust off that bottle because you're going to Grandma's house. It's time to trace the family tree.

This time, however, everything will be different. Rather than letting Grandma ramble on for hours about the hardships of her youth in the Celtic ghetto, you'll be calling the shots. Come prepared with specific questions to lead you down the more interesting path of your family's heritage. Here are some examples:

"Do you know where our family name originates?"
"Who was my great, great grandfather on Grandpa's side?"
"Are we related to any famous people?"
"How is it that Aunt Caroline's baby was born eleven months after Uncle Phil left for the war?"

Other areas that may pique your interest involve your physical hand-

> "The family tree is worth bragging about if it has consistently produced good timber and not just nuts."
>
> **—Glen Wheeler**

me-downs. The pug nose may be obvious looking at your dad, but what about that sloping forehead or the ability to curl your tongue? (Remember eighth-grade biology class?) And although the constant jokes about inheriting your father's chest may amuse your mother with her 44DDs, wouldn't it be nice to have someone in the family to bill for all your miracle bras?

While you're at it, why not find out how Uncle Alan, related by marriage, is the sole member of the clan who is equally as obsessive-compulsive as you? Surely someone at the family reunions is a closet condiment alphabetizer, just dying to move the mustard between the ketchup and relish.

But no lineage grilling would be complete without asking about the black sheep in the family. Everyone has one. After all, the dysfunctional family is as American as apple pie, right? So go ahead, ask the unaskable. Dig for pay dirt on the one relative no one seems to speak of—your transsexual Aunt Norma, a.k.a. The Relative Formerly Known as Uncle Norman. And as Grandma squirms in her housecoat, not knowing that you've secretly already uncovered the story (thanks to Cousin Tammy who has a reputation for big ears and an even bigger mouth), you can sit back and sip your scotch, watching her scour the back of her mind for a suitable analogy:

"Dear, let's just say that Aunt Norma started out as a potato . . . and ended up as a french fry."

Just be forewarned. While such inquiries may leave you itching to talk to your grandmother more frequently, she may stop returning your calls altogether.

Ladies, Start Your Engines!

* **Talk to older relatives who know more history. Ask specific questions or show photos and ask for identification.**
* **Search family members' attics, closets, bookshelves, photo albums, baby books, diaries, Bibles, and so on for clues to your lineage.**

✳ Research censuses, military records, and immigration information at a library or historical society. Each state's Vital Statistics Division of the State Department of Health will usually give you information for a small fee.

✳ Check out some of the Web's best sites:
- Get genealogical organizations listed by state, as well as tips about researching the family tree at www.ancestors.com.
- The National Genealogical Society's website contains library records. Searches are done for a fee at www.ngsgenealogy.org.
- Check out Cyndi's List at www.cyndislist.com, which offers more than 40,000 links, categorized and cross-referenced into 100-plus areas.

44

After the Third Glass, It All Tastes the Same

Attend a wine tasting and learn that there's more to life than screw tops.

If you don't own a corkscrew or you think that complementing a meal with a little wine means telling your food it looks good then adding a nasally complaint, or if you refer to pinot noir as "that nasty French cologne," then it's time to learn more about the finer points of wine.

There are several approaches you can take to understand how to taste, rate, and choose a wine. Although there are plenty of books and videos on the subject, it's often best to get firsthand knowledge by attending a few wine tastings and seminars.

Call your local wine specialty shops or even some fancy restaurants, which sometimes offer free tastings in the hope of attracting new patrons. Wine makers offer free seminars as well, usually on the premise that you'll become a loyal fan, recommending their home brew to friends and family.

Once you find a tasting, be prepared to sample quite a few. You'll probably be given water, bread, or sorbet to "cleanse the palate" between varieties so don't arrive too full to rinse with a few mouthfuls of sourdough. (Then again, don't arrive with such an empty stomach that you'll be dancing on the tables doing your impersonation of Demi Moore in *Striptease*.)

Take small sips of each wine you sample and hold them in your mouth for a few seconds to get the full flavor on your

> "I only drink to steady my nerves. Sometimes I'm so steady I don't move for months."
>
> —W. C. Fields

tongue before swallowing. Take notes of which ones you like or don't like and why. Does the vanilla aroma of the pinot grigio remind you of your childhood? Is the oaky taste of the cabernet sauvignon too overpowering? Does the buttery texture of the sauvignon blanc coat your tongue with a soft, delicious taste leaving you wanting more? Does the cherry flavor of the house red make you want to beat the tar out of the restaurant owner?

Don't be afraid to ask questions at the seminar. That's what the seminars are for. You probably won't be the only beginner, and the more introverted novices will appreciate you acting as their spokesperson. Questions such as "What makes one wine better than the other?" or "What is *tannin*?" are perfectly respectable inquiries. "How many glasses will it take to render me unaccountable for a one-night stand?" and "Did somebody piss in this?" are not.

If you discover a wine that you're particularly fond of, take careful note of the vineyard, the name of the wine, and the year it was produced so that you can stock up for your next dinner party or use it as a last-minute gift idea. Many wines vary greatly from year to year so don't be alarmed if Robert Mondavi appears to have fallen off the wagon in 1996 when the surrounding years produced such fabulous results. (It's hard to run a company from the Betty Ford Clinic—they allow so few phone calls.)

With hundreds of thousands of wines on the market today, there's no reason you can't attend multiple tastings in the same month. (Note use of the word *month*, not *day*.) Your chances of sampling the same wines at different facilities are slim to none unless a local vendor is really earning her keep by pushing the booze in all four corners of the city. Feel free to call in advance to ask about which wines will be presented, and of course, ask if there's a fee to participate. The last thing you want is a bill in your mailbox for an event you can't even remember—like the time you rented that hotel room after the Phish concert in California.

Ladies, Start Your Engines!

✳ To get a head start, pick up a copy of *Wine for Dummies* by Ed McCarthy and Mary Ewing Mulligan.

✳ Find a vineyard near you at Wines Across America's website: www.wines-across-america.com.

✳ Check out the Wine Lovers Page at www.wine-lovers-page.com. Don't forget to sign up for the free weekly wine tips by E-mail!

45

Wieners and Balls

Spend a day at the ballpark and drool over the tight pants and cotton candy.

If crotch scratching and tobacco spitting aren't your idea of a good time, you're really missing out. In addition to being a great pastime for kids and adults, baseball affords today's woman the opportunity to enjoy watching a game with more to look forward to than the chance of catching a fly ball.

First, take the spectacular views. No, not of the oversize billboards in right field. No one cares who's sponsoring the season with free dugout munchies. The other views: Grown men of Adonis proportions are sure to tickle your fancy as they parade their manly butts around the field in tight, well-tailored uniforms. Bring your best binoculars (or telescope for a *real* close look) to place your vote on whether the packaged goods are up to par. (Hey, they do it to women all the time!)

If baseball players aren't your type, scope the crowd. You're sure to find someone worth looking at. And if you can't find someone to daydream about, the beer vendors are always good for a laugh.

Another great addition to your day at the ballpark is the incredible junk food. From cotton candy and freshly popped popcorn to tap beer and hot dogs, few can resist the temptations of stadium cuisine. But be sure to head out with an empty stomach and a full wallet; your day in the sun will make a layover at the airport bar seem cheap.

> "Ninety percent of the game is half mental."
>
> —Jim Wohlford

Besides food you may find yourself dying for some team para-phernalia to remind you of your solo sporty adventure: a banner for your wall, a T-shirt for your cousin, or a big foam finger for your boss (not *that* finger).

Be sure to bring those items that will keep your frivolous spending to a minimum, such as a hat or sun visor (can you believe people still wear those?), a thick sweatshirt or light jacket, and an umbrella or sun-block, depending on your weatherman's forecast. (You may want to bring both if he's known for his inaccuracies.)

You may also want to pick up a brochure showing close-ups of all the players, so you know exactly who you're drooling over if you for-get your binoculars. Wouldn't you hate to find out later that you've been fantasizing about grabbing the ass of the seventy-year-old third-base coach? You may never look at a man in uniform again. Of course, you could always make an exception for the cute E.R. doctor who treats you for a severe case of indigestion. Perhaps there is an advantage to eating five hot dogs.

Then again, maybe next time you can just catch the game on TV.

 Ladies, Start Your Engines!

✳ Brush up on the basic rules of baseball with the book *Spectator Sports Made Simple* by Dan Bartges.

✳ Think you know your stuff? Try your hand at baseball trivia at www.members.tripod.com.

✳ Ready for spring training? Play baseball on-line at www.fansportsnet.com.

46

The Eleventh Commandment: Thou Shalt Not Oversleep on Sunday

Go to church and learn why there's more to Sundays than the funny pages.

Admit it. The last time the "spirit moved you" was when you emptied the contents of your stomach after a night of binging on 100-proof whiskey. Why not try ingesting a different type of spirit by checking out a Saturday or Sunday service? If you haven't been to church or temple or mosque in years and the idea of raking up four trash bags full of dog shit from your neighbor's lawn sounds more appealing, you should know that worshipping is different than it used to be. First of all, you're an adult now. No more getting dragged off in itchy formalwear to sit through three hours of lectures. You choose the place of worship that's right for you. You can even jump around to try out a new one each week until you find one you like (and unlike dating, no one will call you a slut behind your back).

Looking for a traditional service? Try a big ol' brick Catholic cathedral. You'll have the opportunity to cleanse your soul by spilling your guts (without the help of Wild Turkey), and you'll even get to chow down on a wafer before washing it down with a free beverage! Or maybe an Orthodox service conducted in Yiddish is more to your liking.

If you're leaning more toward the left and would rather understand what you're singing about, try a Unitarian Universalist church—they tend to focus more on nature and community service than on biblical teachings. U.U.s welcome *every-*

> **"Worship the gods, listen to their advice, but don't lend them money."**
>
> —Anonymous

one, including gay, lesbian, bisexual, and transgender parishioners, so if you're up for an out-of-the-ordinary sermon and a post-service chat with some varied viewpoints, a liberal church should probably be your first stop.

On the other hand, if you're seeking some fire-and-brimstone preaching where the minister pounds his fist and works up a sweat, a Baptist parish may offer the most comfortable pew; likewise if you're searching for some hand-clapping, dancing-in-the-aisles Gospel music. (This is especially good if you can't carry a tune. Your off-key screeching will be drowned out by the choir—even at a hundred feet away.) Baptist churches are great for lifting your spirits. Just eat your fill before you arrive and don't make plans for the rest of the day, as services often run for hours without breaks.

Or perhaps you're seeking a more meditative style of worship, in which case Buddhism might be the balm to give you inner peace. Still hesitant? Check out the local college campus's student services. The younger crowd may put you more at ease.

No matter which denomination calls your name the loudest, starting your Sunday with a dose of "amens" and "praise Allahs" may give you the three things you can always use: new friends, a renewed faith in spirit, and a sense of belonging. Sure, it may take a year, 50 churches, and several religions before you find a place to call your own, but once you do, you may find that worshipping can actually be fun. Plus, you'll have a great excuse when your neighbor comes knocking.

 Ladies, Start Your Engines!

✳ Not sure what to expect? Pick up a few bulletins from various houses of worship several days before the services to get an idea of what each is all about.

✳ Don't worry about wearing your best dress. Many of today's services, other than the very traditional, are surprisingly casual. When in doubt, wear the equivalent of work attire—but not what you wear on casual Friday!

✳ If you're dressing for a service at a traditional Muslim temple, be aware that some have strict rules about women's clothing, including covering the arms and legs.

✳ Bring a few bucks just in case you get the urge to purge your wallet.

47

Cheerleader Meets Den Mother

Coach a kiddie sports team for the fun of it.

Maybe you were the basketball team's M.V.P. three years in a row in high school or an All-American soccer star in college. Why not put your athletic prowess to good use while you contemplate the possibilities of parenthood by signing up to coach a kiddie sports team? If you already have kids, you may choose to coach one of theirs or a different one. Even if you weren't the first pick for every dodgeball game, willingness and patience account for at least 50 percent in today's busy world when time is as precious of a commodity as a half-caf double latte.

There's probably at least one local team looking for a fearless leader, and you're just the woman to step up to the plate (or the foul line) and take a chance with a bunch of ten-year-old mini–Michael Jordans. Call some local elementary and middle schools and ask if they need a coach in your area of expertise. (Knowing the basic rules of the game may be enough to jump you to the top of the list of "qualified" candidates.) Make sure practice sessions and after-school games fit into your work schedule and be absolutely sure you won't change your mind midseason. Kids become attached to their mentors, and whether they're winning or losing, they'll be aiming to make you proud. Be prepared to schedule your dates around games, unless you're lucky enough to find

> "Everybody knows how to raise children, except the people who have them."
>
> —P. J. O'Rourke

someone who's willing to court you from the sidelines. ("Can I offer you a squirt bottle of Gatorade?")

As for coaching's influence on your decision to have kids of your own, it could go either way. You may find the kids so endearing that you can't imagine a life without a little one . . . or two . . . or three. On the other hand, you may realize just how much you enjoy your privacy, your $200-a-week shoe allowance, and your microwave meals for one. Just be clear about reading the hands on your biological clock. The difference between having a kid of your own and coaching a kiddie sports team is that someone else takes the kids home after the game. If it makes you sad, maybe it's time to start putting something aside for a college fund. If you're thrilled to jump into your convertible and peel out, leaving the minivans in your dust, maybe it's time to beef up your birth control methods.

 Ladies, Start Your Engines!

✻ If you don't want to go through a school, start your own team with a group of kids in your neighborhood. Challenge a friend to start her own team and hold a biweekly district playoff.

✻ Find out what sports aren't covered by your local schools. Create a position for yourself by offering to coach for free. Ask the school to post a sign-up list with a tentative schedule that works for you.

✻ Check with your local YMCA or YWCA to ask if they need coaches for afternoon or evening programs.

✻ Practice with your team. Coaching doesn't necessarily mean standing on the sideline with a whistle. Use the opportunity to get some exercise and prove to the kids that you're as dedicated as they are.

48

My, What a Lovely Set of Canapés You Have

Who needs a partner to throw a swank dinner soiree?

Take a hint already. First you received a Christmas card from Stouffer's, then you cashed in your free, round-trip tickets to London compliments of Domino's Pizza, and now Ronald McDonald has personally invited you to the latest franchise's grand opening? It's definitely time to expand your culinary repertoire.

Sure, you could invite over a slew of friends and relatives to show off your Susie Homemaker skills, but who wants to wait on a bunch of drunken revelers who'll probably end up crashing on your couch and stopping up your toilet? Why not save yourself the trouble of washing ten sets of everything and throw a swank dinner soiree for one?

Think of the possibilities when your budget has to accommodate only one serving of everything: one lobster, one filet mignon, one Kahlúa cheesecake. (OK, two cheesecakes. But you'll make them last the weekend.) You can pull out your best china that's been gathering dust, the linen napkins that are still tied with the original pretty ribbons of some well-meaning Martha Stewart wannabe, and that solitary stem wineglass that survived your move cross-country by mistakenly being packed in your sock box.

Woo yourself with some soft music and a few scented candles while you sashay around the house in nothing but an apron. (Hey, you gotta protect your assets from grease splatters, right?)

> "Sacred cows make the best hamburgers."
> —Mark Twain

Wining and dining yourself has great benefits that dates and multiperson gatherings don't have. First, there's no pressure to "repay" anyone for an expensive dinner. No quibbling over who picks up the tab, no letting down gently when your date expects a nightcap (and then some), and no writing thank-you notes to express your gratitude for "a very enjoyable evening." There's also no chance you'll get stood up, and you won't have to take a taxi home because your date is drunk, obnoxious, or in jail for assaulting the valet. Best of all, you can eat all the food you want, any way you want. Pick up that steak with your hands. Suck the last remnant of meat out of that tiny lobster claw. Have a third helping of chocolate mousse. Drink half the bottle of wine if you want—you don't have to drive, answer to your mother, or consummate the date.

One night of gourmet cuisine probably won't break the bank, but it may be enough to break your pattern. You might find that eating like a queen really suits you. That's not to say that you'll want to give up all your microwave meals and take-out menus. But why not leave that ribbon-cutting ceremony to the clown with big shoes. You've got your own ribbons to cut from around your linen napkins.

 Ladies, Start Your Engines!

Check out these fabulous books and rev up your taste buds:

* *The $50 Dinner Party: 26 Dinner Parties That Won't Break Your Bank, Your Back, or Your Schedule* by Sally Sampson

* *The Dinner Party Cookbook: Menus, Recipes & Decorating Ideas for 21 Theme Parties* by Karen Brown

* *Gourmet Cooking for Dummies* by Charlie Trotter

* *Cooking Light: the Lazy Gourmet*

* *Gourmet's In Short Order: Recipes in 45 Minutes or Less and Easy Menus*

* *The One-Burner Gourmet* by Harriet Barker

49

Hello Mudda, Hello Fadda

Go to summer camp for big girls. Who says you're too old to run away?

Remember how fun summer camp was once you got over the initial anxiety of being separated from your parents for a month? Swimming in the lake, arts and crafts, singing silly songs, and having pillow fights over who'd get the top bunk. Oh, to be a carefree child once again! To be able to leave the doldrums of everyday life in search of the meaning of life at the bottom of a three-ounce cup of "bug juice."

Who says you can't get the same feeling as an adult? There's no rule that says you can't experience the joys of summer just because you've got a car payment and a mortgage. Search for an adult version of your fabulous childhood pastime in the phone book under *retreats* or *camps*, or check the Internet for a woman's retreat within driving distance.

If you still can't find the right resort to relive your childhood experiences, re-create the world's greatest home-away-from-home by signing up to be a camp counselor. Check with some of your local youth organizations to see if they can refer you to any summer camps. If you're skilled in a particular area, such as writing, playing guitar, or painting, or if you're a certified lifeguard or an experienced equestrian, you might get first dibs on a camp staff position. Of course, you won't make much money, but you'll have your housing and meals taken care of for the duration of your stay. And everyone knows there's nothing better than camp food!

> "Happiness is having a large, loving, caring, close-knit family . . . in another city."
> —George Burns

Some camps run as short as one week and if you're due a paid vacation you'll be able to justify the break from your nine-to-five job as a money-making adventure. What other vacation can offer *that* deal? Certainly no one's going to pay you to take a booze cruise, and unless you happen to snap a picture of Elvis at the blackjack table, your odds of coming home from Vegas with a wad of cash are slim to none.

Other advantages of being a camp counselor include bonding with the kids, meeting other adults who love the idea of summer camp, and accumulating a slew of great memorabilia to remind you of your vacation: a walking stick, a homemade birdhouse, a quilted pillow, and if you're lucky, a funky jar of rainbow-layered sand! Even "The Price Is Right" can't compete with those prizes!

If you're one of the unfortunate few who never had the opportunity to attend a summer camp, now's the time to make up for it! There's no statute of limitations on reaping the benefits of relay races, campfires, and flashlight tag, and it's cheaper than dishing out $100 an hour for therapy.

The finishing touch? Write to your parents on your homemade, birch bark stationery. Tell them how much fun you're having and that you only wish you'd had the opportunity to do this as a child. If you play your cards right, they may cave in from guilt and offer to pay for travel expenses to next year's camp—which just happens to be in Cancun.

 Ladies, Start Your Engines!

✳ Find a summer job as a camp counselor by your preferred location at www.campchannel.com.

✳ Consider your budget when applying for a position as a camp counselor. Do you have enough in savings to make up for a meager paycheck? If not, go for a shorter camp or one that's only on the weekends. If you can afford it, be brave and try a monthlong adventure.

✳ What age of kids do you prefer to work with? If you can't take elementary schoolers or teens drive you up a wall, be sure you know what you're getting into.

50

Solo Shutterbugging

What do you get when you mix black and white film with your 1978 Instamatic camera? Probably some pretty kooky pictures!

You see black and white photography in museums, art shows, and highbrow restaurants. Those shots may be taken by professionals, but who's to say *you* can't snap similarly snappy pictures? Sure, those photographers probably had years of artistic training and a camera that costs more than your car, but don't let that intimidate you!

If you are one of those "photographically challenged" people who could use a $5,000 Nikon with a SuperZoomAstroTelephoto lens and still manage to cut someone's head off or get a thumb in the picture, don't give up. Nobody's going to compare your stuff to Annie Leibowitz's work on this week's cover of *Vanity Fair*. Concentrate on just having fun and experimenting, and don't worry too much about lighting, technique, or other stuff you know nothing about. Just load some film, venture out into the world, and see what happens!

While you could go with standard color film, black and white pictures seem to have an artistic, timeless quality that color pics just don't have. Black and white photography hearkens back to the days when tastes were more subdued, and it seems more unique than everyday color snapshots, especially for personal portraits. What's more, black and white film is not too much more expensive than color film, and some brands can be processed at one-hour locations, similar to color film processing. Just expect to wait a week before you get to see your fine pics, even at the "one-hour" place.

> **"If something happens that wasn't premeditated, photograph it."**
> —John Sean

Pictures preserve a moment in time, which can be a good thing (a summer snapshot of you tanned and toned and at the height of your babe years) or a bad thing (the hideous perm you got five years ago, immortalized forever on film). The cool thing is, creating your own "art" photos provides personalized artwork for your home, sparing you from poster-shop bargain-bin rejects. Forget the typical dreary and humorless art photography that often moves viewers to stifled yawns—"grizzled farmer guy standing on windswept plains in dirty overalls" or "single bare branch against a blustery winter sky." Why not go for the gusto! How about these:

* Weird things around your neighborhood. Got an eccentric old lady who walks her big fat bulldog? Ask permission to snap a candid of her and Chugger out on their afternoon stroll.

* The outside of your house or apartment. Twenty years from now you'll have that photo to remind you of where you came from.

* The hunky neighbor who parades around in underwear without closing the curtains first. Practice your stealthy voyeur skills and hope the telephoto lens on your camera works. *National Enquirer*, here you come!

 ## Ladies, Start Your Engines!

* If you're a beginner, sign up for a quickie photography class at your local camera store to learn how to get the best possible shots.

* Don't be afraid to get close to people and objects. One thing you want to keep in mind is filling the picture.

* Play around with different film types—if you're used to using black and white film, why not try some color shots?

* Don't feel like you have to go buy a slew of new camera equipment before getting into photography. The plain-old 35mm you already own will probably do just fine!

51

Girls Kick Ass

Catch on to the exercise craze and get buff.

Have you looked in the mirror lately and found your formerly firm backside looking more like your chubby Aunt Martha's? Here's a scary thought—if you keep putting off getting in shape, it won't be long before the butt you used to flaunt so proudly in skintight jeans becomes a whole lotta jigglin' going on, encased in orange support hose and hidden beneath a pair of elastic-waist, stretch gabardines!

Here's a quick test to help you know for sure if you are out of shape: If you have to lift up a butt cheek with one hand to shave the back of your thighs, you're out of shape. If your formerly flat tummy is starting to bulge enough to rival Uncle Phil's beer belly (and you're punching new belt holes, just like Uncle Phil!), you're out of shape. If, when you put on a pair of panty hose, all the fat gets pushed over the waistband in a violent eruption of ripply flesh, you might want to think about getting a workout plan.

If you want a firm fanny fast, there's always the fitness standbys of jogging or step aerobics. But running more than half a block is tough if you're too far out of shape, and step classes make clumsy chicks feel as though they're bouncing around like an overgrown "Romper Room" reject, constantly tripping over that annoying plastic step. Surely there's a way to get in shape without a size-2 airhead named Brittney in a thong

"When I feel like exercising, I lie down until the feeling passes."
—Robert Hutchins

bouncing up and down in front of you, screeching out instructions over bad, way-too-loud tunes!

Lucky for you there are millions of ways to blast your bod back into shape, and all from the comfort of your own living room if that's what you want. Bikes, cross-training machines, treadmills, stairsteppers, yoga tapes, Pilates routines, aerobics programs, kickboxing—you name it. No matter what you're looking for, there's something for you. If you don't believe that, just think of these weightloss testimonials that any good late-night-TV junky will recognize: "I lost eighty-five inches in a week with my new Super Fat Zapper treadmill" . . . "They used to call me 'double wide' until I caught Tae Bo fever" . . . "I used to stare slack-jawed at the boob tube eating chips by the handful until Denise Austin saved me." Just what you want to hear as you're sitting slack-jawed, staring at the boob tube, eating chips by the handful!

The fitness section of your local video shop is a great place to find the latest exercise tapes. Not only can you try the workout before you invest in a tape, but also most stores have a fairly wide range of choices (sorry, a "Sit, Snack, and Be Fit" video doesn't exist).

Or, take a drop-in fitness class at your local gym or recreation center. Our advice? Go early and stake out the spot behind any hardbody hottie in attendance. Even if you hate the class, visions of tight buns behind oh-so-lucky workout pants should provide ample entertainment to see you through the hour (exercise increases sex drive, you know . . .).

So start working out and sweat yourself into a frenzy in the privacy of your living room or at your local gym. If nothing else, it will help you earn those handfuls of chips!

 Ladies, Start Your Engines!

✳ Ask if you can drop in on a class for a trial run before you pay for a whole six-week session so you can see if you like the music and moves.

✳ Set a weekly fitness goal to help keep yourself on track. Check out websites www.4fitness.com and www.bodytrends.com for motivation and exercise videotape recommendations.

✳ If you don't like the classes offered by your gym, stop in to the free-weight room or try the various machines. And don't be afraid to ask how to use them.

✳ Check the schedule at your local recreation center for women's weight classes. Chances are they're offered a few times a week, and you won't find a better deal.

✳ Rumor has it that if you eat lots of vitamin C after working out, you won't be as sore the next day.

52

Weird Uncle Warren, Crusty Aunt Catherine

Plan a family reunion.

Ever heard the saying "You can pick your friends, but you can't pick your family"? There's a good reason for that. Plenty of people can't stand their kin, and even those families that *seem* perfectly nice and normal can be downright soap-opera-quality dysfunctional at times! Whether you like your family members or enjoy living a thousand miles away from them, a family reunion offers a rare chance to gather together to celebrate the bonds only a family can share.

You may be saying to yourself, "You haven't met my family! The only 'bond' my family shares is the bond we had to post for Uncle Gary's bail when he was arrested for public drunkenness! Why on earth would I want to gather up my motley crew of a clan?!" And to that we say, "Because they're your family, that's why!"

Reunions can be fun—especially if your idea of fun is Aunt Sally's kidney pie, Uncle Bill's lethal whiskey breath, and Cousin Sal's terminally boring girlfriend Candy's nonstop chatter. Seriously, a family reunion is a great way to catch up on distant cousins, bury old hatchets, and reconnect with your past. And every family, like every individual, is unique. No matter what kind of shady, alcoholic, closet cross-dressing, trailer-park trash you call kin, it's nice to be part of something!

As if that's not motive enough, here's another reason to plan a family reunion: You'll get to find out about any strange,

> **"Insanity runs in my family. It practically gallops."**
> —Cary Grant,
> Arsenic and Old Lace

debilitating diseases that run in your family! Plus, check out how your mom and the rest of the elder generation look—it'll be like looking in a mirror twenty-five years from now!

If you decide to take up planning a family reunion, pick a date far enough in advance to give everyone plenty of notice. It might be good to call around to find out if there are any weddings or vacations planned that would keep people away. If it's to be a small gathering, host it at someone's house and make it a fun summer barbecue. Enlist the help of any siblings or cousins to gather phone numbers and addresses so you can let everyone know about the reunion. If you have a large family, plan to hold it at a resort, park, or entertaining spot—you'll get extra points for picking a fun locale, since the time can also serve as a sort of vacation.

After the planning is done, sit back and prepare yourself for the unsolicited advice, backhanded compliments on your choice of attire, and questions about your current single status and/or the details of any new love affairs, along with reminders of at least two embarrassing things you did in childhood. Do yourself a favor and get these all out of the way in the first hour. Then you can relax and dig in to the eye-popping buffet your awesome family set up!

 Ladies, Start Your Engines!

✳ Take lots of pictures if the clan doesn't get together often. You don't want to miss this golden photo opportunity.

✳ Pass around a blank address book and ask everyone to fill in addresses and phone numbers. Then offer to make copies for everyone, so folks can keep in contact.

✳ Invite everyone, even the family members you know can't make it—it's still nice to be invited.

53

High-Estrogen Filmmaking

Rent chick flicks on a Friday night.

If you'd rather watch the grass grow than sit through a guts-and-guns
testosterone Arnold farce, you'll love this idea: set aside a Friday night
and rent a stack of chick flicks!

When guys use the phrase "chick flick," they usually guffaw and
roll their eyes. But what exactly is a *chick flick*? Burt and Kindberg
define a chick flick as "any movie with a bunch of female characters
sitting around talking about sensitive stuff." You know, lots of emotion,
love stories, family dramas, women of many generations, and so forth.
They are often accompanied by a gushy soundtrack with lots of airy
violins and have plenty of the soft-lensed beach shots you see in
douche commercials, with a few wizened granny figures thrown it for
good measure.

Of course, no chick flick night would be complete without other
stereotypical feminine trappings! Why not enjoy some light popcorn
and diet soda along with your movie? Or, a bottle of "white zin" perhaps? Don't forget to cozy into the couch with fluffy pillows, a mani-
cure set, a cordless phone, and tissues nearby, just in case.

If you're usually not a chick flick fan, give 'em a chance. They aren't
all about repressed housewives or
"three generations of women in a pic-
turesque Midwestern town talking
about hysterectomies." The worst that
can happen is that the blood-and-guts
stuff might not look so bad after all!

> "I just love, I love, I love movies."
>
> —Laura Dern

Here are a few titles to get the tears rolling:

* *Thelma and Louise*: Susan Sarandon and Geena Davis star as two feisty southern women on a crime spree in a really cool car.

* *Waiting to Exhale*: Four successful African American women living in Phoenix struggle to find true romance as they weed out the losers.

* *Steel Magnolias*: This comedy/drama with Sally Field, Dolly Parton, and Julia Roberts is about southern women sharing triumphs and tragedies in a beauty salon.

* *The First Wives Club*: Bette Midler, Diane Keaton, and Goldie Hawn star as middle-aged jilted wives plotting revenge against their husbands.

* *Fried Green Tomatoes*: This is a rural sentimental portrait of the friendship between two feisty women in a small Alabama town.

* *How Stella Got Her Groove Back*: Angela Bassett stars as a divorcée who relocates her groove by carousing on a Jamaican beach (and hotel room!) with a Jamaican stud half her age.

* *Chippendales, Tall Dark and Handsome:* This is a hardbody beefcake review. (Just seeing if you were paying attention!)

 Ladies, Start Your Engines!

* Ask the clerk for chick flick suggestions. There might be some great obscure flicks you've never heard of!

* Get comfy in your slippers and pj's before you start.

* Check out www.filmgeek.com for reviews. This website is rated "The best reviews you'll read on-line and off" by the L.A. *Times.*

54

Come On, Baby, Light Your Own Fire

Learn to hand dip candles.

OK, ladies, pop quiz: It's Saturday night, and you're expecting company in five minutes. You glance around the apartment that your roommate forgot to clean (it was her turn this week!), and notice lint clinging to the carpet and dust an inch thick in your living room. What do you do?

A. Speed clean like a madwoman hopped up on Pine Sol fumes, pushing that Dustbuster to maximum capacity.
B. Scrawl a quick, angry note to your roomy that reads, "Thanks for cleaning the living room, bitch!" and leave it on her bed, prompting an all-out catfight when she gets home.
C. Dim the lights to "erase" the carpet lint and dust, then ignite a few candles to add atmosphere.

If you answered C, congratulations! You're a savvy hostess (and tolerant roommate) who knows that the flicker of candlelight adds an instant glow that can help turn a cluttered little corner into a cozy cove and glosses over the flaws of a cleanliness-challenged room.

Chances are you already worship the wick for its many wonderful qualities—heck, you'd practically have an altar full of candles burning away in every room if you had it your way! But if you've ventured into a candle store lately, you've undoubtedly noticed that what used to be

> "It is better to light one small candle than to curse the darkness."
>
> —Confucius

simple pillars and plain old tea-lites have turned into sophisticated triple-wicked affairs. It's easy to walk into a candle store and blow quite a few bucks, only to get a measly bag of vanilla votives and some boring beige tapers. The solution? Make your own candles!

If laboring over a vat of hot wax sounds as appealing to you as scrubbing your kitchen floor with a toothbrush, take heart—once you get the supplies together, it's simply a matter of melting the wax, adding fragrance, and pouring it into the mold. Voila! You'll save money and have candles in the exact color and fragrance you like. Practically every craft store in the country offers books on the subject, along with all the wicks, waxes, and fragrances you'll ever need. Most even stock candle-making kits with all supplies included—perfect for the novice who wants to try her hand at the craft without buying a truckload of paraffin.

As for your roommate, the next time she forgets to pitch in, threaten to use her gourmet copper-bottomed double boiler to melt your candle wax!

 ## Ladies, Start Your Engines!

✳ Check out www.candleandsoap.miningco.com and www.craftcave.com for advice and supplies.

✳ Try mixing various scents for candles that are truly unique. Who says you can't mix vanilla, lavender, and rose?

✳ To get wax remnants out of a candle holder, run it under hot water to soften the wax, then gently chip the wax off with a knife.

✳ Check out *Candle Creations: Making and Arranging Candles for Beautiful Effects*, a gorgeous book by Simon Lycett, the guy who created the fabulous arrangements in *Four Weddings and a Funeral.*

55

Everything Old Is New (and Chic) Again

Do a funky refinish job on an old dresser.

Dying to put a little dazzle in your decor? The good news is, you don't have to be Martha Stewart to have a cute pad. The bad news is, efforts to decorate often end up something like this:

1. Sift through the latest copy of *Architectural Digest* and *Elle Decor* for decorating ideas, gazing longingly at the exquisite furnishing displays.
2. Close the magazine and glance around your own apartment, noticing the 1974 wood paneling, the ratty couch, and the dust-covered entertainment center with a broken cabinet door. Flop down on the ratty couch in disgust and disappointment.
3. Sulk in front of the TV the remainder of the night, watching old "Decorating with Bea Smith" episodes.

Well, don't give up hope yet! The key to building up your confidence at decorating is to start small. It's as easy as slapping some funky paint on an old dresser or nightstand! A little paint and some imagination can turn any piece of dusty, plain-Jane furniture into an attention-getting conversation piece that will perk up an entire room.

The first rule to refinishing a dresser or chest is that there are no rules. Whether you prefer a subdued single shade or go for a wild color combo that resembles a paint store explosion, getting started is half the work. The beauty of painting a dresser is that your finished piece will

> "It's a good thing."
> —**Martha Stewart**

be beautiful and functional (and you probably already own a dresser that can serve as your palette). And the beauty of paint is that you can paint over something that isn't up to snuff. That's a relief when you find that the Warm Golden Chestnut paint that looked so good in the store actually looks more like Dog Shit Brown.

While there are no rules, there are a few things to remember to minimize headaches later. Choose furniture manufactured from wood, rather than plastic or wood laminate. Paint bonds to wood best and can be sanded off if you wish to return a piece to its former state.

Experts will probably tell you to sand off any existing finish, apply a primer coat, use only high-quality paint, etc., etc., but who has time for that?! You're trying to create funky furniture, not become a master woodworker! We say grab any old brush, pick a few colors you like, and let the splatters fall where they may.

 Ladies, Start Your Engines!

✳ Check out TV shows on decorating for inspiration and ideas. Discovery Channel's "Christopher Lowell Show" and Lifetime's "Next Door with Katie Smith" offer upbeat decorating advice.

✳ Search through the "mis-tint" and discounted paint bin at the local hardware store. These paints may have been mixed to the slightly wrong shade by store clerks and can be snatched up at a fraction of the cost. Paint recycling centers also sell cheap paint, but the variety of shades may be limited.

✳ Remove hardware such as hinges and knobs before you start. Don't try to "paint around" hardware. (We all know that *never* works!)

✳ Buy extra paint. You don't want to run out halfway through the job, then go to the hardware store to find out the paint you need has been discontinued. And if your color is one that has to be mixed in the store, chances are no two cans of paint will match exactly.

56

High Prose, Black Berets, and Beatniks

Read poetry in a spunky coffee shop.

Wanna make Jack Kerouak proud? Dress in your best black leotard 119
and matching beret and head to your local bookstore or coffee shop for
an evening of espresso, top-notch literature, and the intangible auras
of obnoxious aloofness.

To find out what it was like to be part of the 1960s pseudo-
intellectual underground, schedule your night of roleplaying to coin-
cide with an open-mike poetry reading. As an observer, be sure to snap
your fingers in lieu of clapping at the end of each poet's share session—no matter how torturous the listening experience is.

If you're feeling daring and would like to try your hand at reading,
but you don't really consider yourself a poet, take the easy way out by
sampling from some text you already have. No, not Shakespeare's greatest hits, but rather the back of your shower gel bottle. "Brimming with
lavender, tempting your senses with the tantalizing scents of nature,
treat yourself to the soothing indulgence of life's pleasures." Who'll
know the difference? Just don't put your name to it or you may get
sued by Johnson and Johnson.

If the bubble bath label doesn't roll off
your tongue, try another approach: the
label from your tea sampler. Rearrange
the words from the label, adding a mix of
your own creativity. "Nature's herbs, sharing your sweet chamomile, soothe me

> "An intellectual snob is
> someone who can listen to the
> William Tell Overture and not
> think of 'The Lone Ranger.' "
> —Dan Rather

with your, aromatic pleasures that I may curl up in your, toasted almond arms." Now who'd boo Lipton?

If a poetry reading isn't your cup of tea, browse the bookstore shelves and gather a stack of books that would normally be too expensive to purchase on your thrift-store wardrobe budget, then head for the nearest comfy chair in the corner. Feel free to hide a trashy magazine inside your stack of Thoreau, Whitman, and Tolstoy. If you keep your back to the wall, you'll look like a savant whipping through a pile of classics, while you catch up on your free doses of *National Enquirer* and *Playgirl*.

No matter what your taste, today's bookstore is the way to go for free reading. Sure, the library's nice, but why not get the same browsing privileges with the added benefit of caffeine and chocolate? No library is going to allow anything more than chewing gum and trips to the water fountain, and who wants to leave the premises for a bite to eat, just when you've found the Ricky Martin centerfold?

Perhaps you could browse through the entrepreneurial books to brush up on your business skills. You may want to open your own bookstore-slash-restaurant some day—where patrons can dine on seafood scallopini while they devour *Moby Dick* and the only thing in the black will be your bank account.

 Ladies, Start Your Engines!

✳ Curious about the Beat generation? Check out any of the works by these writers:
- Jack Kerouak
- Allen Ginsberg
- Robert Creeley
- William S. Burroughs

✳ Here are more books to give you some insight:
- *Women of the Beat Generation* by Brenda Knight
- *Beat Spirit: The Way of the Beat Writers as a Living Experience* by Mel Ash

57

Do Not Disturb

Rent a room for the night.

Renting a room. . . . Oh, the pleasures of hotel-supply-store artwork
bolted to the walls, daily maid service, the minibar, the toilet paper
folded to a little point. A girl could get used to this! Best of all, staying
alone means no one to hog the remote or pout if you feel like watching four hours of "Laverne and Shirley" reruns. And no one but you
cluttering the tiny bathroom vanity with razors and cheap aftershave.

Even cheap motels have a certain fun and funky charm. Where else
can you experience the sounds of an old man in the room next door
hacking up a lung over the sounds of CNN cranked up way too loud?
It's great to stay where the only dishes are individually wrapped plastic cups, and the only phone calls to annoy you are the curt desk clerk
placing your morning wake-up call.

Too bad people usually rent a room only when they're on the road,
having a clandestine fling, or getting the floors redone in their own
house. Staying in a motel is a cool change of pace when you need a
change of scenery (especially if that scenery includes a chatty roommate who never seems to go anywhere!). House a mess? Decor getting
you down? Get away for a night! Cable
is always better when broadcast on a
TV bracketed to the wall, wouldn't
you agree?

If you have the bucks, go to a
deluxe bed-and-breakfast for a real

> "A hotel is a place that keeps the
> manufacturers of 25-watt bulbs
> in business."
>
> —Shelley Berman

minivacation. The top-end places feature featherbeds, piped-in chamber music, antiques galore, plus a mouthwatering gourmet breakfast in the morning. Check B&B guides for one near you.

Of course, you could slum it and go to a cheap motel! Just don't slum it too hard—cheap doesn't have to mean unsafe. If you notice bullet holes in the windows patched with duct tape, and no other cars in the parking lot, that's a bad sign! So are rooms that rent by the hour.

Once you've checked in, here are a few things to do:

* Read a trashy novel like *Valley of the Dolls* by Jacqueline Susann.
* Order a large pizza delivered to your room and scarf down the whole thing.
* Vegetate with old sitcom reruns, like "Happy Days," "Wings," and "Scooby Doo."

 Ladies, Start Your Engines!

* Bring plenty of quarters for the vibrating bed and the vending machines, in case you need some emergency potato chips.

* Don't forget a bottle of champagne for the ice bucket.

* If you're a pillow snob, bring your own from home. Once you've gotten used to sleeping on cushy down, it's hard to snooze on cheap polyfill.

* Be naughty and swipe the "Do Not Disturb" sign.

58

Biker Dudes and Cycle Sluts

Hop on a Harley and haul ass to the Sturgis Motorcycle Rally!

Has this ever happened to you? You're sitting at a stoplight in your dorky two-door, when up rumbles some bad-ass dude on a slick black motorcycle. He's covered in leather and studs despite the blistering heat, the sun glistening off the chrome and reflecting onto his beefy, chiseled arms. The light turns green and he tears off down the road, wild hair flapping in the wind and skull tattoos fading into the distance. You smile in envy of such a wild and free spirit.

It's time to hop on your bad motorscooter and ride, sister! That could be *you* tearing down the road, and you don't even need the skull tattoo to do it (unless you want one, of course). Become one of the millions of bikers that cheat death, feeling the exhilaration of sheer horsepower as a ton of hot metal vibrates beneath you, screaming down the highway at ninety miles an hour! You can join the ranks of biker chicks everywhere by riding an "iron horse," and all it takes is learning how—and shelling out some serious bucks for a motorcycle and equipment.

Before you get all revved up about the idea, sign up for a motorcycle safety class through your state's Department of Motor Vehicles (which also issues motorcycle licenses) or local motorcycle shop. You'll learn crucial motorcycle-riding techniques that can make the difference between arriving at your destination and ending up a stain on the highway. Many programs provide

> "It's one thing to have people buy your products. It's another for them to tattoo your name on their bodies."
> —Harley-Davidson website

bikes for participants, so you'll have to buy only a helmet and accessories to begin. It's also a great way to try before you buy—motorcycles aren't for everyone, and you may discover the only bike you're comfortable riding is the ten-speed Schwinn you've had since high school.

Once you've become a budding biker babe, why stop there? Unite with other motorcycle fans across the country by hopping on your hog and rumbling up to Black Hills, South Dakota, for the annual Sturgis Motorcycle Rally! (After all, what good are leather chaps if you can't show them off?) The Black Hills Motor Classic is in its sixtieth year, attracting more than 250,000 bikers annually to the event. The rally features motorcycle races, displays of everything new in the motorcycle world, concerts, lots of interesting, hairy guys, and tons of biker chicks struttin' around in leather miniskirts. What could be more fun?

So strap on some leather and get going! And next time somebody pulls up next to you in a dorky two-door, be sure to flash 'em your best bug-encrusted grin!

 Ladies, Start Your Engines!

✳ Check out the Sturgis website at http://rally.sturgis.sd.us or write for more information to

> Sturgis Bike Week, Inc.
> P.O. Box 189
> Sturgis, SD 57785

✳ Don't have the time or cash to go to Sturgis? Visit your local leather store and try on the leather duds for an afternoon. And don't forget to strike a few tough-chick poses.

✳ For all of the thrill with none of the potential brain spill, play a motorcycle racing video game instead—no helmet required!

59

Venus on the Fairway

Tee off and polish your golf game at the local driving range.

Golf is such a dignified sport. You've got to love any activity that's **125** called a sport yet doesn't require heart-pounding aerobic activity and sweat rolling down your forehead. Plus, where else but the golf course can you wear the traditional pom-pom hat and plaid knickers and *not* look like a clown school reject? All this, and a gorgeous setting, too. Golf courses, especially the snooty exclusive ones, have grass greener than AstroTurf and breathtaking landscaping, with all sorts of fountains and ponds dotting the rolling hills.

If when you think of golf you picture a bunch of overprivileged white guys in sport shirts negotiating corporate mergers between holes, you may have a distorted view of the game. More women are going ga-ga for golf than ever before, and it's attracting more young people, too. Credit Tiger Woods and Adam Sandler's movie *Happy Gilmore* for making golf hip among Gen Xers. These days, you can even buy golf shoes that aren't hideously ugly (unlike those of yesteryear that looked more like bowling shoes with teeth).

Next time it's a lovely spring day and you're thinking of heading outdoors, go golfing! You don't have to tackle an entire eighteen-hole course to get into the swing. Consider going to a driving range instead. A driving range is sort of the Cliffs Notes of a full course, with a row of places to stand and hit balls into a

> "My swing is so bad I look like a caveman killing his lunch."
> —Lee Trevino

field for swing practice and the chance to say, "Hey, I hit that one pretty damn far!" They'll have all the clubs and balls you need. So why not drop by on a long lunch hour, hit a few balls, and blow off a little frustration from that 10 A.M. meeting?

Or how about a little miniature golf? Don't laugh! Miniature golf may seem totally ridiculous to "real" golf players, but it's still a fun way to get in a little putting practice. Plus, even in towns where there's no golf course around, there's probably a putt putt. And where else can you experience kitschy minigolf fixtures like the slow-turning windmill or the tiny cement "pond" they built on the last hole?

Whatever you choose, do your fellow golfers one favor—look behind you before you swing the club.

 Ladies, Start Your Engines!

✳ Golfing comes with its own set of protocol and etiquette. Check out the United States Golf Association's website at www.usga.org for conduct tips, so you don't make a "golf faux pas" on the green.

✳ Little-known fact: The spin rate of a golf ball when hit by a driver is approximately 3,600 revolutions per minute.

✳ Rent the movie *Happy Gilmore* if you think you're taking this whole golf thing too seriously.

60

Beauty School Dropout

Talk yourself into a new hairdo.

Having a bad hair year? Every woman hates the realization that the glorious glowing tresses that should be her crowning glory are actually frizzled, icky spindles of hair—not even hair, dried up hair stumps.

Have you ever noticed a woman and thought to yourself "she'd be so cute if she would just fix that God-awful hair"? Well, guess what—people might be saying the same thing about you! You think you look cool until you see a picture of yourself. The hairdo you thought said "windblown waif" actually says "washed-out white trash" and the cute, short cut you thought accentuated your cheekbones has you looking like your great-aunt Louise—all you need now is your once-a-week roller set and a plastic rain scarf tied firmly at your chubby chin!

Bad hair happens to everyone at some point. (Remember Cher's frost-tipped mohawk in the '80s?) The good thing about hair is it grows out. Bust out of hair purgatory and quit waiting—waiting for the day when your hair grows into the cool style you've always wanted, waiting to outlive a bad perm, waiting for the color job to fade. Wake up and smell the awapuhi creme rinse! Take your locks in hand and march into the toniest salon in town for a totally new 'do!

You may be tempted to go to the five-dollar Thrift-T Cut, but don't do it. A total tressular transformation requires expert help and the advice of an experienced stylist, not the amateur effort of some

> "You're only as good as your last haircut."
>
> —Susan Lee

flunky from Konnie's Kut Rate Barber Kollege. Sure, you'll pay through the nose, but it's your hair, damn it! And unlike an ugly shirt or a bad pair of shoes that you can get away with once in a while, there's no hiding a hideous hairdo. You need a salon, baby! Go where the shampoo boys are dressed better than you, there's a monthlong wait for an appointment, and the hair gel costs more than your car payment.

If you aren't sure where to go, ask a well-coiffed friend who does her hair. Hairdressers love referrals, and it's a good way to know whether the stylist does good work or not. If you already like your stylist but just want a new look, give your old stylist a chance to work magic on you. She's probably been biting her tongue about your outdated style for years and can't wait to transform you into the babe you know you are!

Not sure about what look will be a "look" on you? If you think your hair would look cool short, blond, and sassy, pop into a wig store and go crazy! Most clerks will let you try on a few styles hoping you'll buy something. Better yet, check out some of the makeover software on the market. Simply scan in your headshot and superimpose all sorts of fun styles.

Or, simply live with the look you've got. Hair stumps are bound to be in style someday!

 Ladies, Start Your Engines!

✳ Take your dream hair on a test drive with makeover software, like Cosmo's Virtual Makeover.

✳ If you get a bad haircut, try to carry it off by telling everyone "it's supposed to look this way!"

✳ When all else fails, throw on a hat—hair problem solved!

✳ Take a picture of your desired haircut in to show the stylist. That way she'll see exactly what you mean by "short and spiky."

61

Host a Friday Office Bash

Organize a Mexican food potluck for your office.

Welcome to another week. You know the drill: Bummer-It's-Monday **129**
is followed by Too-Stressful-Tuesday and Snagged-My-Hose-Wednes-
day, which brings you to Two-More-Days-Till-the-Weekend-Thursday,
and finally Thank-God-It's-Friday.

That's life in the office until you die or retire, whichever comes first.
Shouldn't you be having more fun, especially since you spend most of
your life at your job? You may be trapped toiling away in a nondescript
little cubicle just waiting for five o'clock, but why not shake up the
office a bit? Offer to host a Friday potluck at your work for your fellow
cube dwellers! Break out of the "another Friday spent at Burger King"
routine and invite your coworkers to join you for a Friday Mexican
Fiesta Gorgefest sure to knock your colleagues on their tamales.

But you hate your job, you whine. Your coworkers are dull, humorless slobs that require nerves of steel to endure for even an hour-long
staff meeting, much less to actually eat lunch with them. That's exactly

why you should host a potluck! Lure
your coworkers away from the safety
of their little offices with some tasty
guacamole, and you just might find
that Sally from Marketing shares
your passion for dark chocolate and
"Cops" reruns. And Boring Bob from
Accounting? He's still boring, but he's

> "The brain is a wonderful organ.
> It starts working when you get up
> in the morning, and doesn't stop
> until you get to the office."
> —**Robert Frost**

nice, and he might surprise you by bringing a fabulous casserole. You won't know till you invite him!

A potluck is the perfect excuse for slacking off: "Sorry I wasn't at my desk, I had to set up the conference room for the potluck." "No, I can't take a call. I've got nacho cheese in the microwave." "I know I'm late, but I had to pick up some paper plates." The possibilities are endless!

Here's how it works. First, ask your boss if it's OK to use one of the conference rooms or common areas to host your little shindig. Argue that a potluck will build morale and that salsa will strengthen the camaraderie among coworkers. You might even score points with the boss for being proactive and a team player. (You don't need to tell her you're

just doing it because you're bored at work and heard that the new administrative assistant used to be a chef and makes the best damn enchiladas on the planet.) Assuming your boss isn't a total ogre and says yes, post a festive sign-up sheet in the break room announcing the potluck, and ask coworkers to sign up to bring a dish.

Divide your sign-up sheet into five categories (main dish, dessert, drinks, side dish, or salad) and put two or three lines under each category. That way you'll have a well-rounded menu instead of ten lazy coworkers all showing up with a bag of chips. Try to include lots of politically correct choices such as meatless entrees and kosher choices so you don't leave anyone out. Make sure you have all the bases covered on the sign-up sheet. And don't forget the napkins, utensils, and such—there's nothing worse than trying to spoon nacho cheese onto chips with a flimsy little plastic spoon!

 Ladies, Start Your Engines!

✳ Send all your coworkers a reminder E-mail the day before the potluck to make sure they bring the food they signed up for.

✳ If office policy allows, bring a portable radio with some happy fiesta tunes to play at the party.

✳ Invite departments other than your own so you can get to know others within the company. Now's your excuse to chat with the hot newbie who works in the mail room!

62

Touring Anywhere, USA

Sign up for a tour of your hometown.

Whether your town has a population of one thousand or five million, **131**
it's the place you call home. If you just rolled in from somewhere else,
or if you've lived there all your life, there are bound to be things about
the city that even you don't know. Why not educate yourself by taking
a tour of the city through the Chamber of Commerce or the Tourism
Office? A city tour is a pleasant way to spend an afternoon and a great
way to get the skinny on Scranton, the poop on Podunk, the dish on
Dirkville.

The whole idea barely solicits a yawn, right? Wrong! Not all city
tours are boring. Sure, usually the tour starts out with the predictable
details of how your town sprang up out of nowhere and which formi-
dable founding father was responsible for putting it on the map. But
some tours slip in all sorts of kooky details and quirky history to liven
it up. Even sleepy little Midwestern towns have their share of drama.
You could find out a whole slew of stuff about your town that makes
it all the more interesting of a place to call home. Here are some
possibilities:

* The historic loft building downtown that is now the Christian
  Coalition League used to be a
  whorehouse at the turn of the
  century.

> "A small town is a place where
> there's no place to go where
> you shouldn't."
>
> —Burt Bacharach

* His Honor Mayor Thomas Wilby used to lock the door to his office and dress up in women's underwear. A city councilman once walked in on him squeezing into a corset-and-thigh-high number!

* Ever wonder why the county border is crooked? The county commissioner designated the border after a liquid lunch.

* Ever noticed that the city's handsome young attorney general is the spittin' image of Governor Groemer from the 1950s? Rumor has it he's the illicit love child of Governor Groemer and state secretary Sally Tinsdale!

Know what else is cool about taking a city tour? You'll learn enough history to make you a pretty good guide yourself when visitors come to town. Now when your parents fly in and you're trying to figure out how to entertain them, you'll have something to do—without yet another trip to the museum or popping for $100 tickets to Riverdance at the Performance Center. Just hop in the car, have your parents sit in the back, put on your best tour-guide voice, and tell them all about your new hometown. They'll appreciate your effort, and maybe they'll be so impressed with your city knowledge that they'll finally quit bugging you about moving back home.

It'll be the last time you hear your mom wishfully mutter, "This city is too big, noisy, and dangerous for my little girl! Why don't you move back home, dear? You know, Ricky Shelton is assistant manager at Main Street Hardware now. He's not married! He still asks about you. . . ."

 Ladies, Start Your Engines!

* Call your city's tourism bureau for details on tour dates, times, and prices.

* If you live in a city near the water, inquire about bay or shoreline tours, where you kick back in a boat rather than schlep around on foot.

* If you live in a small town that doesn't have city tours, take a tour of your history museum instead for a double dose of education and culture.

63

Entrepreneur 101

Turn a hobby into a business.

Surely you've seen the Cinderella success stories of entrepreneurs who launched a new business and achieved wild success with a former hobby. You know, the ones where some guy started out as an anonymous cube dweller until he started making Widgywigs in his basement. Next thing you know he's President and CEO of Worldwide Widgywigs, raking in dough hand over fist, his boring corporate job a distant nightmare. Why can't that be you?

Even if you love your "day job" and can't imagine doing anything else, it's always fun to have something on the sideline! Hobbies make life interesting, especially weird pastimes (that means you, jug band members and emu breeders!). You have to pay the bills somehow, but most gals have a creative passion that they pursue in their free time. Are you a company middle manager who works out the stress of the day by throwing pottery at night? Possibly a sales manager trapped in the body of a weekend gardener? Even a toll-booth clerk who loves to belt out a snappy jazz tune when no one's around? Well, don't hide your light under a bushel basket—share it with the rest of the world. You might be surprised where it takes you. The world needs more closet jazz singers, budding basket weavers, and would-be Appalachian dance cloggers!

> "You may be a redneck if you think you are an entrepreneur because of the 'Dirt for Sale' sign in the front yard."
> —Jeff Foxworthy

Do it before you start thinking, "Oh, why waste my time trying to launch a side business? Nobody's going to want to see my poems /paintings/songs/photos/cartoon drawings! Boo hoo, the world is so tough on us delicate creative types. Woe is me; I shall never be appreciated for my creative genius. Alas, I'll just toil away quietly in obscurity, and save my hobby for my own enjoyment."

That's stinkin' thinkin', sister! Nobody says you're gonna buy a BMW with the proceeds from your basket weaving, but wouldn't it be fun to maybe make a buck or two and meet some fellow basket-weaving buddies? Don't think your stuff is good enough to show, sell, or otherwise share with others? Even if your family thinks you're insane for your love of ShrinkyDinks, there are people out there who would love to see your collection. Maybe you could organize a local confederate of ShrinkyDink fanatics, and you can all trek off to some exotic locale to attend the National "Shrinkypalooza" Expo!

All it takes is the courage to branch out a little and start thinking with a marketing bent. If you have a craft you'd love to sell, take a few around as samples to little shops in town and ask to sell them on consignment. If you're a budding writer or photographer, go to the library for books on where to send your stuff (how do you think this book got started?). Better yet, publish your own book and skip that whole nasty rejection mess! If your thrill is a talent like acting, dancing, or singing, put your head together with others and start a performance troupe or community performance group. Even gardeners can put together a plan to sell their talent as consultants to give green-thumb tips to the botanically challenged. Backyards everywhere need your expertise!

 Ladies, Start Your Engines!

✳ Start reading mags like *Entrepreneur* and *Small Business News* to feel like you're part of the "entrepreneur club."

✳ Call your state's Secretary of State or Commerce department. Some states have set up small-business resource centers to help newbie business owners with everything they need to get set up.

✳ Check out www.entrepreneur.com for all sorts of cool tips.

64

Looking for a Good Baba Ganouj

Explore new culinary frontiers in the ethnic food markets.

As the world gets smaller and global influences invade our palates, there's a whole dimension of strange new tastes awaiting the adventurous eater. From Middle Eastern to Ethiopian to Vietnamese and Thai, from Scandinavian to Jamaican, open your mind and your tastebuds will follow.

Still there are plenty of ladies whose taste in food is strictly American. If your idea of an adventurous meal is Tabasco on your meatloaf instead of ketchup, you're overdue to expand your culinary horizons! A dish of phad thai, mutton murtabak, or baba ganouj is what you need to keep your tongue on its toes!

The fun part about buying food in ethnic markets instead of just ordering from a restaurant is that you can cook it yourself and adjust the taste accordingly. If the curry Akee at the Jamaican joint down the street leaves you burping spicy reminders for half a week, make it yourself with a little more Akee and a little less curry. Plus, shopping around is a great way to get introduced to new ingredients you might not try when ordering off a menu.

Here's a rundown of a few market types to get you noshing internationally:

Middle Eastern: Middle Eastern markets often carry products from a variety of countries, including Morocco, Greece, and Egypt. Look for deals on falafel

> "I didn't fight my way to the top of the food chain to be a vegetarian."
>
> —bumper sticker

mixes, fresh pita bread, feta and goat cheeses, and the best damn selection of olives you've ever seen! FYI, because of the Islamic influence in Middle Eastern countries and Islamic rules against consuming pork or alcohol, asking where the link sausage and Miller Light are won't win you any friends. If that happens, pick up a copy of the Koran to score brownie points with the clerk.

Asian: Authentic Asian markets ain't for the squeamish! Westerners will see row after row of items they've probably never heard of (squid ramen noodles, dried snack fish), and the live seafood selection in tanks is sure to blow anyone away (fresh ink squid, anyone?). The good news is that you can find some pretty interesting produce and a huge variety of teas, spices, delicate cookies, and serving ware. And try the squid—you just might like it.

Mexican: If your idea of Mexican food is the Taco Bell nachos grande, go straight to a Mexican food store, chica! Mexican and Latin American markets offer more chiles, mole sauces, chocolates, and baked goods than you can shake a tamale at.

If you wouldn't know a murtabak if it bit you on the ass and don't want to look like a Big Dumb American, don't be intimidated! Most clerks are friendly and willing to answer any questions you might have. Besides, where else are you gonna get seasoning tips for frying fresh ink squid?

 Ladies, Start Your Engines!

✳ For you fancy feast types, check out www.epicurious.com or www.gourmet.com for killer recipes with ethnic foods.

✳ Live in a small town without much ethnic food action? Ask your local grocer to order in specialty items for you.

✳ Many ethnic stores also carry housewares and general items—if exotic food just isn't your style, it's still worth a visit to pick up a funky teapot or glass set.

65

Immortalizing Fluffy

Videotape your pet for posterity.

Hairballs and vet bills aside, few joys can compare to pet ownership. **137** Whether it's a one-hundred-pound bull mastiff named Duke, a five-pound kitten named Snowball, or a six-foot anaconda named Beauregard, pets each have a unique personality, just like people. What other creature is kind enough to curl up on your pillow despite your morning breath and gobble down dessert disasters without complaint?

When Fido goes on to the Big Doghouse in the Sky, don't let the only images you have of him exist just in your memory or plain old photographs. Videotape your buddy running, barking, and being adorable. Those video images will last for years to come and you just might catch him doing a kooky trick that'll win you thousands of dollars on "America's Funniest Videos." Plus, taping your pets instead of your friends means you won't have to endure complaints about looking ten pounds fatter on camera.

Taping your pet should be pretty easy if you have a dog or a cat. Most of the time, they're prowling around barking or meowing anyway, so they make great subjects. It's the "alternative" pets that might be a little harder to get a good video of. Let's face it, there's not much thrill in shooting thirty minutes of videotape of your iguana perched motionless on his heat rock or watching your fish swim endless loops in

> "A dog wags its tail with its heart."
>
> —Martin Buxbaum

their tank. How about shooting them at feeding time to coax a little movement when you shout "action!"?

You could also liven things up with a little narrative—to break the silence. "Here's my pet piranha Squishy, purchased from Petland down the street. I call him Squishy because he's not much fun to cuddle with." Or, dress up your pup in a cute costume and get him to parade around your kitchen while you give viewers the fashion fine points: "Rocky looks ready for action in a kicky pink and black rhinestone collar and fuzzy acrylic doggie sweater, a must-have for fall."

Need more ideas? Set up a stealth taping mission and film pets with a hidden camera to solve the mystery of which of your cats has been peeing on your carpet. Or, when something's been snatching snacks off the kitchen counter and you aren't sure who's the culprit, you'll have the evidence to convict on first degree kitty mischief! And cats, unlike dogs, can see the TV screen—just pop in the evidence tape when they start meowing in protest their claims of innocence and rubbing against your leg in a plea for leniency.

Ladies, Start Your Engines!

- **Bribe your pooch to smile for the camera by baking him homemade treats! See www.twodogpress.com for yummy recipes.**
- **Don't let your pets lick the camera lens—dog slobber is hard to wipe clean from the glass!**
- **Get your pet a cute new collar or sweater for its big film debut.**

66

Stogie Suzie Meets Humidor Helen

Kick back and have a cigar in a posh cigar bar.

Feel like hitting the town but don't feel like slumming it? Dump your local dive for a change and hit an upscale, downtown kind of place— somewhere where the music springs from a tinkering baby grand piano instead of a rickety jukebox spewing "Achy, Breaky Heart" and the drinks aren't served in forty-ounce bombers (not to knock Colt .45, by any means). You might really dig the sophisticated atmosphere and even meet a few guys that have names imprinted on business cards instead of their belt buckle.

The best part about posh bars? The cigar room in the back! Love it or loathe it, cigars are in—at least that's what *Cigar Aficionado* magazine says. So jump on the bandwagon and fire up a stogie, sister. Unlike plain old cigarettes and their image as stinky sticks chock-full of cancer, cigars evoke an image befitting leather chairs, pinstriped suits, and dry martinis. Not that you have to wear a pinstriped suit and sip a martini to enjoy one. In fact, if you like the whiff of cigars but don't want to smoke 'em, just lounging in the cigar room taking in the secondhand smoke is almost as satisfying as being the primary puffer.

Plus, the fact that cigars are meant to be savored rather than inhaled the same way cigs are—and if you indulge only occasionally—you'll be able to keep that pesky lung and throat cancer at bay while you contemplate a fine hand-rolled

> "A good cigar is as great a comfort to a man as a good cry is to a woman."
>
> —Edward G. Bulwer-Lytton

Cuban. Unless you make cigars a lifelong habit, chances are you won't keel over on your way to the car, so live a little! Hey, it worked for George Burns, didn't it? Any habit that comes with this many rules and protocol can't be so bad.

Don't feel awkward about being a cigar virgin, either. Most cigar rooms sell a wide variety in varying prices and categories, and the counter stewards hopped up on secondhand stogie smoke simply can't wait to give you a crash course in the fine art of cigar smoking, answering such burning questions as: How do you choose a cigar? Why do you cut the tip off? How do you keep it lit without sucking on it constantly? How do you smoke it without slobbering like a beagle?

The best way to find these posh cigar lounges is to hang out downtown or patronize tony establishments catering to high-class clientele. And don't forget that gold pinky ring if you really want to fit in!

 Ladies, Start Your Engines!

✳ If there's not a cigar bar in your town, just light up where you live and stink up your own place! OK cigar smoking with the landlord first, though.

✳ Did you know cigars come with accessories? It's true! Visit a tobacco shop for humidors, cutters, and other cigar-related goodies.

✳ For all of the fun of cigars with none of the lung disease, collect antique cigar boxes and funky lighters instead!

67

Instant Harmony Through Feng Shui

✳

Explore the ancient oriental art of feng shui and reap the rewards of a harmonious environment.

Fired from your job? Boyfriend dumped you? Fighting a yeast infec- tion from hell? Don't go blaming your ill tidings on your boss, or boyfriend, or polyester panties, for that matter. Blame it on foul feng shui instead!

Feng what, you say? *Feng shui* is the ancient Eastern art of creating a harmonious environment through object placement. According to fans of feng shui, arranging your home and grounds in a manner that promotes a positive flow of life energy (also known as *chi*) can make a world of difference in countless little ways, just as ignoring basic feng shui rules can bring unfavorable results. In fact, good *chi* is pretty much given credit for all sorts of things, from a healthy bank account to a booming career to a zippy sex life. And while the whole idea of *chi* and energy flow might sound a little like a New Age snake oil pitch, feng shui has certainly garnered a lot of attention lately—and it can't *all* be b.s.

Feng shui involves using shapes, colors, and other factors to attract *chi*. If it sounds complicated, it is. Here are a few concepts behind feng shui:

✳ Don't display cut or dried flowers; dead equals loss of vitality.
✳ Wind chimes and bells can be useful in dark corners and long corridors where they attract and invigorate *chi*.

> "Better to do good at home than to go far away to burn incense."
> —Ancient Chinese Proverb

✳

* Red is deemed to be auspicious, be it a red brick house or a red flagstone walkway to your front door. Filling up your garden with red and yellow flowers in a flowing pattern is a good idea.

* When gardening, avoid coffin- or tombstone-shaped plots. Evergreens on the property line secure longevity. Do not plant anything near the front or the back of the house, as this will block *chi*.

* The entry of your home or office should be open and inviting, so trim away foliage that may be blocking the path of *chi*.

* Keep bathroom doors shut, with toilet seats down, to prevent *chi*, opportunity, wealth, and happiness from being flushed.

* Avoid having sharp, pointed buildings, wall corners, furniture, or accessories pointed directly at your house, bed, or desk. It is reminiscent of a cutting knife edge or a disapproving finger.

* Use all five traditional elements (fire, wood, metal, earth, and water) in your design for energetic emotional and decorative balance.

Scads of books exist on feng shui, so pick one up. If you're a little skeptical, check a book out from the library rather than buying it. To really understand the concepts behind feng shui, enroll in a short course or adult education class. A few hours with a knowledgeable teacher and that *chi* will be whipping around you in no time!

 Ladies, Start Your Engines!

* Get a copy of the book *The Complete Idiot's Guide to Feng Shui* by Elizabeth Moran and Val Biktashev. Also check out *Feng Shui Goes to the Office* by Nancilee Wydra for tips on making your workspace more productive.

* If you rent your place and aren't allowed to paint the walls, hang a large colorful sheet or cloth wall-hanging with plain thumbtacks to create instant good vibes.

* If you're too lazy to rearrange and paint, hang some wind chimes in strategic places. They sound great and look cool, too!

68

Surfing and Splurging on the Internet

Log on and break out your credit card.

This World Wide Web hubbub is moving at an explosive rate! Isn't it **143** funny that with all the high-tech networks of computers and space-age satellite technology employed in launching the Internet, most people use it just to buy stuff and download porn? You could be using the Internet for deep and meaningful exploits, like researching world religions, locating lost loves, or buying some really cool shoes!

The benefits of Internet shopping are infinite. You can by stuff at 2 A.M., when every other retail store has long since closed. And the variety is mind-boggling, whether you're shopping for books or bras, clothing and accessories, groceries, concert tickets, vitamins, red wine, CDs, makeup and toiletries, you name it! Plus, shopping on-line saves time—no more trucking down to the mall, fighting traffic, and wrangling with overly aggressive sales clerks!

Even gals living in Small Town, USA, can purchase stuff usually found only in big cities. A pair of thigh-high leather Gucci boots are sure to attract attention with the old ladies at the 4-H booth at the Podunk County Fair!

Other than having to wait for your stuff to be shipped to you, the only bummer about Internet shopping is having to use your credit card. All the sites *say* they are secure, but there's still that nagging feeling some techie geek halfway across the country is somehow

> "Credit cards have three dimensions: height, width, and debt."
> —Shelby Friedman

magically downloading your credit card number and charging a twin box set of *Star Trek Revisited* and *The Babes of Star Trek*. Just stick to sites that guarantee your privacy and security and you should be fine.

Here are some cool sites to start with:

Drugstore.com: health, beauty, wellness, and pharmaceuticals delivered to your door. Plus a free e-newsletter!

eBay.com: a whopping auction site, selling just about everything, including computers, figurines, dolls, collectibles, automotive supplies, and electronics. Sell your own stuff here, too.

Mothernature.com: vitamins, supplements, and herbs for great prices.

CDnow.com: a mind-boggling selection of CDs and cassettes. If CDnow doesn't have the CD you want, it doesn't exist.

Shoes.com: the shoe superstore, with brands like Birkenstock, Mephisto, Rockport, and more.

Really cool shoes halfway across the world await you!

 Ladies, Start Your Engines!

✳ Check your favorite sites regularly—many of them offer dollar-off deals and coupons, but they often expire without notice.

✳ For more about Internet splurging, check out *The Best of Online Shopping: The Prices' Guide to Fast and Easy Shopping on the Web* by Lisa Price and Jonathan Price or *Bargain Shopping Online* by Kate Shoup Welsh.

✳ If you're wondering if a certain site is fly-by-night, before you hand over your credit card number look them up on www.bizrate.com, which is sort of a privately owned Better Business Bureau for Internet sites.

69

Prospects Are Good

Go West for gold panning.

Did you know that prospectors in this day and age still pan for gold in the valleys and hills of the American West? Well, "there's gold in them thar hills," and plenty of it still sits unmined, waiting for one lucky prospector to come along. Nowadays, people pan gold more for fun and to satisfy their Yosemite Sam urgings than to make an actual living.

For you city gals who don't know the first thing about gold panning, here's a quick lesson: *gold panning* is similar to *gold digging*, but you mine for riches with a tin pan in an icy Rocky Mountain stream rather than in some old guy's bank account. Gold panning is a lost art performed mostly by hearty outdoors types who enjoy the mountain air, not people seeking a fortune like the prospectors of yesteryear. Prospecting still requires patience and an uncanny sense of how to discover gold, but even if you don't strike the mother lode, it's worth spending a day outdoors.

What would you rather do—spend a day watching the grass grow or standing in an icy stream with a sluice box and pick? OK, spending hours sorting gold dust from pebbles found at the bottom of a stream isn't exactly a party waiting to happen, but here are some things about gold panning you may not have considered. For some reason, prospecting attracts mainly men, most of them the nature-lovin', grizzled,

> "There's gold in them thar hills."
> —Unknown

bearded types who wear lots of flannel and can build a fire with two wet sticks—if it's mountain men you're itching to meet, get ready to strike it rich! Plus, you might get lucky and hit a fairly sizeable nugget. Whether you decide to cash it in or melt it down for jewelry, the fact that you found it yourself makes it all the sweeter. There's also the boon of trekking around the hills in leather waders carrying a pick axe. Now how often do you get to do that?

If you're a flatlander, chances are you will have to head to the hills to do any prospecting at all. But if you live in a mountainous area, finding supplies and information is easy. Start by calling your local gemstone shop and ask if they know of any prospecting clubs or tours operating in your area. Or, check out the Internet for prospecting information—you'll be surprised at how many people are involved in this little-known hobby!

 Ladies, Start Your Engines!

✳ Call Gold Prospecting Adventures at 1-800-596-0009, or check them out on-line: www.goldpanning.com.

✳ If you're interested in gold-mine tours, look into California's Show Me the Gold tours at www.showmethegold.com or North Carolina's Thermal City Gold Mine at www.huntforgold.com.

✳ Even if it's hot outside when you leave the house, *dress warmly*, especially if you're headed for the hills. The mountains and streams can get very cold—there's a reason mountain men always wear flannel.

70

Wayne's World, Minus Garth

Host your own cable show. Anyone can get on community access television!

If you're one of those people who's convinced that all TV is evil and there's nothing but crap on today, community access television might be right up your alley. Ever been flipping through the stations late at night and run across a Russian talk show or an amateur belly-dancing exposition? That's probably the community TV channel you came across, beaming out strange entertainment, local happenings, and wacko viewpoints to anyone who happens to be channel surfing.

Community access TV is operated by community-based, nonprofit groups who believe in the all-American idea of promoting free speech in the media. Anyone can be on community television, including you! Most don't edit, preview, or take any editorial control over the content of a show, resulting in what could euphemistically be called a mixed bag.

You name it, there's probably a show about it somewhere on community TV. Sure, shows like "Bible Thumping with Bob Green," "Equal Rights for Aliens," and "Shape Up with Yukon Clog Dancing" may not garner gobs of fans and off-the-chart Nielsen ratings, but niche programming does have an audience—even if the only people watching "Bible Thumping with Bob Green" are Bob's wife and kids.

It's remarkably easy to get started, too! The only requirements are that you're a resident of the city in which the community TV station broadcasts and

> **"Imitation is the sincerest form of television."**
> —Fred Allen

that you fill out the application and choose a timeslot. The shows are usually produced by volunteer staff who handle the cameras, lighting, and sound. All you need to do is find out when volunteers are available to help you make your show a reality and launch your career as a huge star. Better yet, become a producer volunteer to learn the ropes of television production—it will help you understand what's going on with your own show, and you might get so into the community TV vision that you end up working on other shows as well.

Psyched up to do your thing but aren't sure what kind of show you'd like to do? Now's your chance to showcase a talent, right a wrong, or spout your left-leaning view of the world. Pretty much anything goes. (Sorry though, playing your thirty-minute rendition of "chopsticks" on the piano won't do—not even your mother wants to be subjected to that!)

 ### Ladies, Start Your Engines!

Here are some wacky ideas to get you started:

✳ First Date Fiascos—host a talk show and gab about the guests' hellish first-date experiences.

✳ Jug Band Jam—now's your chance to give your all-girl jug band the exposure it deserves!

✳ Homemade Soap Opera—write a screenplay for a torrid soap opera, and have your friends act as characters in the pilot episode!

71

Thelma and, uh . . . Thelma

Take a road trip in a rented convertible.

Whether you ragtop it for an afternoon of running errands or a cross-country road trip, driving is more fun when you pop your top! The wind in your hair, the sun on your shoulders, cool tunes on the radio—there's nothing like cruising in a convertible.

149

If the only wind you've experienced lately is your boss's onion breath as he barks orders at you, you're due for a little time off to hit the road! Feign an illness, pack your sunscreen and road map, and blow town in a rented convertible. It'll be just like *Thelma and Louise*, sans Louise. It's probably better alone anyway—you won't have to put up with a too-chatty sidekick bent on a crime spree, and you won't have to drive off a cliff at the end of your trip!

Don't try getting the thrill of a ragtop with the sunroof on your puny little four-door import. Sorry to break it to you, but sunroofs don't count. In fact, trying to glean the glee of toplessness with a sunroof is like trying to get that "gorge on death by chocolate" experience from a dried-up fat-free brownie. Splurge and go rent a ragtop, already!

But before you start digging out the cat's-eye shades, a little pre–road trip work is in order. Look through the phone book, call around to find a rental agency that rents convertibles, and make a reservation. Unfortunately, most car rental agencies don't

> "Men read maps better than women because only men can understand the concept of an inch equaling a hundred miles."
> —Roseanne

handle convertibles, and they are in incredibly high demand, especially in the summer months. If you find one available, snap it up. Or take matters into your own hands and beg convertible-owning friends or relatives to lend you their wheels for a day.

Once you've got your wheels, the radio is playing your favorite song, and you're on your way outta Dodge, where to? Driving in the city can be fun, but the traffic, noise, and exhaust can crush your groove in a hurry. Somewhere with plenty of natural beauty is a great choice. (Be on bird shit alert, though—that's a little too natural!) Nothing beats a cruise through the Rocky Mountains in the summer or through the towering pines on a road through the Pacific Northwest. Even the good ol' Midwestern plains when the corn's tall can perk up your spirits and make you feel like a country girl. Or get away from the city's light pollution and experience the country at night.

 Ladies, Start Your Engines!

Here are a few fun routes to get you going:

✳ Southwestern Utah, near Bryce Canyon and Zion National Park—the stunning canyon vistas will blow you away!

✳ Route 100 in Vermont, stretching from the Canadian border to Massachusetts—make this trip in the fall to check out the foliage.

✳ Pacific Coast Highway in California, from Monterey heading south. The wind, the waves, the lure of Hollywood—just don't pull a James Dean and flip the car while checking out the scenery, or the waves won't be the only thing crashing.

✳ The classic kickin' Route 66 road trip—it starts in the Midwest and takes you west across the country.

72

An Appetizing Whodunit Story

Attend a murder mystery dinner.

There's been a murder in your town. Was it Colonel Mustard in the
conservatory with a wrench, or was it Miss Scarlet with a candlestick
in the dining room? Attend a murder mystery dinner and find out!

Murder mystery dinners add a dash of whodunit and intrigue to
your dining experience . . . kind of like playing Clue while enjoying a
frozen pizza! If you've never been to a murder mystery dinner, it's a
pretty simple concept: You enjoy a lighthearted mystery play while
enjoying dinner. The actors roam through the dining room while
doing their scene or perform solely on stage, depending on the venue.
It's usually held in a dinner theater setting, but occasionally it's in an
upscale restaurant (dinner theater is no fun in a dive, where the only
mystery is what that slimy thing in the salad is).

The awesome thing about murder mystery dinners is that the action
goes on while you're eating. That's particularly good news if you're not
really into theater! Plus, mystery dinners provide entertainment
beyond just the food being served, so you might not mind eating
mediocre chicken marsala if the play is especially scintillating. Don't
forget to chat with your table mates dur-
ing the breaks to try to solve the mystery
by piecing together clues from the first
few acts. The actors sometimes serve
courses between scenes, staying in character while they sling hash and drop

> "It's one of the tragic ironies of
> the theatre that only one man
> in it can count on steady
> work—the night watchman."
>
> —Tallulah Bankhead

murder clues to patrons at the same time. (Actors who double as waiters . . . now *that's* a new concept!)

Feel like grabbing a little spotlight of your own? Most plays make use of audience participation, enlisting the acting skills of diners for cameo roles in the play. Don't worry, though. You won't be called upon to participate unless you volunteer. Wallflowers will be happy to know that they can sit quietly if they wish, chomping away on dinner rolls undisturbed by the thespian goings-on.

To join the fun, try dressing up! Since "all the world is a stage," why not dress for it? The actors are sure to be dressed to the nines to represent their character, so why can't you? Get into the act by sporting a vintage trenchcoat à la Ingrid Bergman in *Casablanca*. Or don a jaunty little velvet hat with a touch of veil covering one eye. Don't forget the long black gloves!

You might enjoy the evening so much that you decide to come back accompanied. Got a blind date you're dreading? Go to a murder mystery dinner! The focus will be on the play rather than on struggling through an awkward, boring conversation about pet hamsters, your date's thrilling job as a corporate accountant, or the weather. Even if the date's a bust, the murder mystery dinner is sure to be loads of fun. But the primary suspect could be you—after you kill your friend for setting you up with such a dork!

 Ladies, Start Your Engines!

✳ Call around for prices before you make a reservation. The prices of some of the mystery dinners can be a real killer (pardon the pun).

✳ Ask theater-loving friends and coworkers to recommend a good show.

✳ Pick up a copy of the Arts and Entertainment section in Friday's newspaper for the latest theater listings.

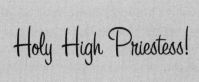

73

Holy High Priestess!

Get ordained in something.

Wouldn't it be nice to be able to make a little extra cash by marrying   153
your best friend? No, not by cashing in on a nice insurance policy after
slicing the brake line in the car, but by performing the marriage
ceremony!

That's right, you too can become a minister for the low, low intro-
ductory price of . . . FREE! (Or nearly free.) Seriously, you can become
a minister. Just sign up through any number of programs, and you'll
be baptizing babies, blessing sinners, and exorcising demons with the
best of them! Imagine how much money you could have spent paying
to go to seminary or all the time you could have wasted actually attending a convent for years on end! Becoming a minister today can be as
simple as the lick of a stamp.

But why all the hoopla over a title that's so easy to obtain? In addition to the monetary benefits, you'll have a front-row seat to heaven!
You'll be leading the choir on the bus ride to the Pearly Gates, reading
scripture (or at least Rumi poetry), and comforting those who had to
leave their less worthy loved ones at the escalator going down.

Until then, reap the benefits of your framed certificate by getting
out of previously unavoidable situations:

* No more horrible bridesmaid
dresses! You'll be decked out in
a slimming black robe, which
can be matched with any of

> "I would have made a good pope."
> —Richard Nixon

your existing shoes. No need to dye those uncomfortable white pumps to a nauseating shade of sea-foam green or mango orange. (And who will know if you don't wear anything under your robe in 100-degree weather?!)

* Scare off unwanted dates by flashing your certificate to annoying suitors. Claim that although you're not Catholic, you have taken a vow of celibacy against having sex with people who remind you of Saturday Night Live characters.

* Get the good parking spots! Just pop your clerical certificate into your front window and slide into otherwise unavailable spaces. No God-fearing meter maid would dare write a ticket to a reverend!

If nothing else, you've got a conversation starter at your next cocktail party. Just watch the eyes bulge when you show up in your robe, Bible in hand, to perform a self-submerged baptism—in the bowl of Sangria.

 Ladies, Start Your Engines!

Write to any of the following for information:

* The American Fellowship Church
  225 Crossroads Boulevard, Suite 345
  Carmel, CA 93923
  ($20 fee; founded in 1975)

* Minister Credentials
  Universal Life Church
  601 Third Street
  Modesto, CA 95351
  (Founded by Kirby J. Hensley in the early '60s. Reverend Hensley ordained the Beatles, George Burns, Wolfman Jack, Betty Ford, Merle Haggard, and Lawrence Welk!)

* World Christian
  P.O. Box 8041
  Fresno, CA 93747
  (Requested offering of $42)

74

A Peaceful Proposition

Join a two-week international peace camp.

Who hasn't thought at one point or another, "I should do something meaningful to help the human race." Such lofty aspirations usually surface while toiling away at a pointless task in some anonymous cubicle or enduring an hour-long Monday commute in 100-degree heat.

Lots of good-hearted people have thought about joining the Peace Corps, but they are daunted by that pesky two-year requirement. The Peace Corps demands a lot of even the most well-meaning people. (Hey, you're good-hearted, but not *that* good-hearted!)

Good news, socially minded sisters! Opportunities abound for short-term "volunteer vacations" that combine doing good work with having a good time. Two-week volunteer expeditions are as personally fulfilling as they are fun (who says you can't build beach huts and work on your tan at the same time?). These kinds of trips are becoming more popular than ever, and they take place in practically every country on the globe, including the good old USA. As a volunteer, you will work with scientists and all sorts of other interesting folks, making you part of a decidedly international crowd. Whether your passion is to nurture orphaned babies in Bangladesh, research monkey mating habits in Panama, or excavate an archaeological site in a Middle Eastern desert, there's a horizon-expanding experience awaiting you.

> "We can say 'Peace on Earth,' we can sing about it, preach about it, or pray about it, but if we have not internalized the mythology to make it happen inside us, then it will not be."
> —Betty Shabazz

155

The choices are overwhelming: nature conservation, social change, animal rights, archaeology, and cultural studies just scratch the surface of stuff you can do. To find the best fit, consider the kind of work you want to do and the kind of place you'd like to visit. Are you as much a sun lover as an animal lover? Studying marine life while diving in the Caribbean sounds like the perfect sojourn! Looking for a culture-shock thrill and want to help impoverished women and children? Help deliver maternity health supplies and educational materials to villagers in Africa!

There are several organizations that can help you discover the volunteer vacation that's right for you. A great place to start is with Earthwatch, a twenty-five-year-old organization matching volunteers with science and conservation projects worldwide, going to far-flung destinations on practically every continent. Earthwatch publishes a gorgeous full-color catalog describing available expeditions throughout the world, all typically running two weeks. Earthwatch's catalog describes accommodations, the type of work you'll be doing, and the required fitness level. They handle all the details, as well as the expedition costs (usually from $1,000 to $3,500), which cover food, lodging, transfers, translators, and local transportation. Call 1-800-776-0188 or see www.earthwatch.org for information.

Global Volunteers follows the same basic concept as Earthwatch, but this group focuses more on social change and education than on nature and animal conservation. Global Volunteers doesn't have the flashy catalog—or the wide-reaching scope—of Earthwatch, but their two-week stints are just as grand, and they go to plenty of exotic places, including Tanzania, Costa Rica, Jamaica, Ireland, and Ecuador. Global Volunteers' enthusiastic staff are happy to send you literature, and they will even put you in touch with past volunteers who can give you the skinny on certain expeditions. Call Global Volunteers at 1-800-487-1074 for details.

Volunteers for Peace is a great place to start if you're looking for bare-bones, get-back-to-nature types of expeditions. Volunteers for Peace operates as a clearing house for local service givers and publishes a directory of two-week work camps in a bevy of countries, many of them very reasonably priced and catering to the college-aged crowd.

Ladies, Start Your Engines!

✳ See Volunteers for Peace's website (www.vfp.org) for a current listing of work camps.

✳ The majority of work camps take place during the summer, so schedule vacation time accordingly.

✳ If you're interested in building homes during your two-week adventure, see Chapter 7 to get the lowdown on Habitat for Humanity.

✳ Ask for names and numbers of former volunteers who've ventured out on such expeditions, and find out what kind of an experience they had.

75

Girls Just Wanna Have Fun

Break out the spandex and throw an '80s party.

Oh, the '80s! From parachute pants and headbands to big hair and leg-warmers, the '80s is a decade best put behind us, at least from a fashion standpoint. What can you say about an era in which skintight pants cut off the circulation of an entire generation, and hair was only cool if it towered a foot off your head, sprayed into place with the stiffest hair goo imaginable? Pay homage to that glam look of yesterday by throwing an '80s party!

Are you thinking "An '80s party? Gag me with a pitchfork! The '80s were horrible enough for me the first time around. Why would I want to relive that?" Maybe you were voted 1984's Least Popular Chick in High School. Or, perhaps you weighed 400 pounds and were ridiculed for it. Or you had to be hauled to the orthodontist regularly because you kept locking braces with Joe from Geometry. Plenty of us were geeks in the '80s and hated every minute of it! But you're all grown up now and doing great, so why not be a good sport and indulge in a little good-natured thumbing of your nose at the decade?

An '80s party is a great excuse to break out all those cheesy albums stashed in your attic and try to squeeze into that pair of frosted jeans you refuse to get rid of. Pair it with something hot pink or one of those fake red leather Michael Jackson jackets with a million zippers for a total trip back in time! Here are a few

'80s Trivia Question: What was Adam Ant's real name?

Answer: Stuart Leslie Goddard

more ideas to get the Pogo Ball rolling: Stress to your guests that it's an '80s party and to dress accordingly—only spandex and painted-on jeans will gain entrance! If you don't tell them to dress in costume, they'll either not be in the spirit or they'll wonder why on earth you are dressed like a *Flashdance* extra with feathered hair.

If you were of high school age during the '80s, break out the Peach Schnapps for old-times' sake (beverage of choice for underage drinkers!). Schnapps tastes like candy but contains enough alcohol to knock you on your ass, as '80s prom queens everywhere can attest. You might even find your guests making out in the coat closet!

The party music is crucial if you want to set the right mood. Play Pat Benatar, Loverboy, Def Leppard, Go-Go's, Adam Ant . . . if you've kept your old albums from the '80s, all you need is a turntable and you're set. If you don't have old albums but want to spin some '80s tunes, most record stores have cheap compilation CDs like *Big Hits of the '80s* to get the party started.

If you really want a night to remember, hunt down some of your old friends from the decade. Contact your school alumni association or try your luck with the phone book and gather up the old gang. You just may find that the hunky football player you had such a crush on is now a fat, balding used car salesman, and the cheerleader bitch who made your life hell lives in a trailer park on the outskirts of town with six screaming little brats!

Throw a smashing shindig, and your guests may even vote you "Like, The Most Totally Awesome '80s Party Hostess Ever."

 Ladies, Start Your Engines!

✳ The '80s weren't your favorite past decade? No problem! Pick another decade with cool props, like a '20s flapper party or a '50s sock hop.

✳ Visit thrift stores for old '80s albums, clothing, and other memorabilia.

✳ Rent *Pretty in Pink* featuring '80s idol Molly Ringwald, *Desperately Seeking Susan* starring actress extraordinnaire Madonna, or other classic '80s flicks to play in the background.

76

The Truth Is Out There

Set up camp at Area 51 with your telescope and video camera.

If you're convinced that every "X-Files" episode is based on true-to-life conspiracies and government cover-ups, you've probably already been compelled to visit Area 51. The Roswell, New Mexico, hot spot has been an attraction to believers and naysayers alike—with both hoping to put a definitive end to their endless pursuits of the truth.

Why not confirm your own truth by heading out for a week at Alien Central? Pack up your best "Star Trek," "Get Smart," and David Duchovny gadgets and head toward the bright light. Must-haves include a tape recorder, a telescope, a camcorder, a camera, and tons of film. Don't forget a sleeping bag for a night under the stars (if they are in fact stars!). You don't expect E.T. to show up at high noon, do you?

With any luck you'll have your name in the Little Green Men Diner right next to the Gupelston twins who in 1967 were either abducted by a race of interstellar beings or experienced their first and final LSD hallucination.

Even if you don't get to climb on board, a quick pic of a metallic disc may be enough to earn you a few grand, or, at the very least, your photo on the cover of *National Enquirer*. Be sure to get a background object, such as a tree, to show size comparisons and light density. It'll be hard to convince a major magazine to cough up cash for a blip of silver on a background of blackness.

> "The truth is out there. So what are you doing here?"
>
> —Anonymous

Looking to pass some time during your visit? Talk to some of the local yokels about their own experiences or those of others in the town. The older the storyteller, the more tall tales they'll have to share about happenings since the 1947 "incident." Take a few hours to research the local library's stacks of stories, the likes of which are rivaled only by the tourist brochures.

You'll want to keep your eyes, ears, and mind wide open to possibilities without looking for something that's not there. The greatest place on Earth to see an unearthly creature may also be the most popular place to pull a practical joke. Just because the locals are open to out-of-this-world visitors doesn't mean they'll take kindly to out-of-towners. Be wary of the flying saucers that still have apple pie crumbs on them.

 Ladies, Start Your Engines!

✳ Check out the world's largest and most complete UFO website at www.ufomind.com.

✳ Everything you need to know but shouldn't! Visit www.area51.net.

✳ Wanna spook yourself? Rent or buy *Area 51—Alien Interview* on video.

✳ Or read *Area 51* by Robert Doherty.

77

Memories of Slip 'n Slide

Start a collection of old toys.

Remember those carefree days of toddlerhood, when your biggest
decision was whether to have Cap'n Crunch or Count Chocula for
breakfast? The only rules you lived by were pummeling your little
brother for tattling on you and making sure you picked up your toys
before bed.

You're all grown up now, and times have changed! Your little brother
is now six-feet, two inches and living in Cincinnati—you couldn't pum-
mel him if you tried. All your fun toys have been replaced with boring adult stuff like blenders, toasters, a VCR, your outdated stereo
system. No adult toys are made of six shades of neon plastic or do anything cool like spurt goo, spin in a circle, or shriek wildly. No wonder
kids think adults are all a bunch of humorless, stone-faced fogies! The
only roller coaster most of us have ridden lately involves the stock market or a rebound fling with an ex-boyfriend.

Well, until the line at the DMV has monkey bars at the end of it, or
Chase Manhattan Mortgage accepts Monopoly money, you'll just have
to inject more fun into your life wherever you can. Reclaim that mis-
spent youth by collecting old toys!

Remember Weebles? "Weebles
wobble but they don't fall down."
Those adorable cone-shaped little tottering people could spin and wobble
forever. And who could forget the

> "Whoever dies with the most toys
> wins."
> —bumper sticker

EZ Bake Oven, which heated up to a whopping seventy-eight degrees and trained little girls into thinking, "Hey, since I'll be slaving over a hot stove for the rest of my life, why not start now?" Remember the little plug-in candy fondue set? It came with its own candy fondue bricks that bubbled into an unworldly cherry-flavored goo that was an unsettling neon pink. And then there was Operation. Trying to remove that damn wishbone out of the plastic patient without that dreaded BUZZ was such a challenge!

·Don't feel silly collecting old toys—especially since all these games have adult uses! For instance, Weebles make great cat toys. They aren't edible, and cats can't figure out how the damn things keep wobbling. EZ Bake Ovens barely heat up enough to warrant plugging them in, but cram a muffin in there and warm it up as you wax nostalgic. The fondue set? That's easy—it makes the perfect wax warmer when it's time to tackle that bikini line! And Operation? The pinchers make good tweezers in case of an emergency eyebrow job.

Best of all, there's Slip 'n Slide—the big plastic sheet that gets hosed down in the sprinkler. Kids take a running start onto the slick sheet and go shooting across the lawn at warp speed. With a little imagination, a partner, and an extra large tube of K-Y jelly, Slip 'n Slide converts into a very adult game!

 Ladies, Start Your Engines!

✳ Most old toys are not on the market anymore, with the exception of Operation, EZ Bake Oven, and Slip 'n Slide. If you see them at garage sales, flea markets, or thrift stores, snap them up.

✳ Some old toys are considered serious collector's items. Vintage Pez dispensers from the '50s can go for more than $200 at a collector's auction!

✳ If you're reliving your childhood and decide to set up the Slip 'n Slide in your perfectly manicured backyard, take note: the plastic kills the grass underneath the slide.

78

Bare Your Ass for Art's Sake

Model nude for an artist and be immortalized on canvas.

The female body is a work of art. Those lips, those eyes, those hips! **165** Admit it, each of us has secretly caught a glimpse of ourselves in the mirror after a heavy primping session and bragged inwardly, "That's right, I still got it!" That said, why not show it off while you still have it?

Immortalize your body by posing nude for an artist! Pose naked today, and tomorrow when you're wrinkled and your boobs hang down to your knees, you'll take comfort knowing there's a piece of artwork out there that commemorates your younger, perkier bod. You'll be in the fine company of women like Mona Lisa or Venus di Milo.

Artists have looked to the nude female form for inspiration for hundreds of years. Ever been to the art museum and left the Renaissance painting exhibition wondering if women ever actually wore clothes back then? They painted naked women sitting by the stream, naked women reclining on velvet sofas, naked women carousing with cherubs with guts and butts hangin' out all over the place!

You may be thinking, "My thighs! My jelly butt! There's no way in *hell* I'm posing nude!" Well, get over it—the female form in all variances of thinness and chubbiness is admired and held in awe by artists. Renaissance painters considered rotund females to be total babes! If you can stand still long enough to stop jiggling, you'll be a natural poser.

> "Life is a great big canvas, and you should throw all the paint on it you can."
>
> —Danny Kaye

Drop by an art school and ask if they use nude models for their classes. Many art schools and college art courses use models in some form for painting and sculpture courses. You may even get paid for your trouble—some schools pay nude models $10 an hour. You can also check the bulletin boards at art supply stores. Many artists seeking models advertise by putting up a notice or placing an ad in alternative papers.

Before you drop your drawers, be sure you're truly baring it all for art's sake and not as whack-off fodder for some creep. Ask if he or she has worked with female nudes before, and look at portfolios of work before agreeing to disrobe. And it goes without saying, the posing should be done in a studio or other artistic setting. Posing nude alone in someone's apartment is a really, really bad idea.

And finally, suck in your gut and start practicing poses that show off your bare assets.

 Ladies, Start Your Engines!

❋ Warning: If you're planning on running for president, this is probably a bad idea.

❋ It's the artist's job to make you look good, but don't be afraid to suggest poses or props that you feel might work.

❋ Ask where the artist is planning on showing the finished piece, if at all. You might not want a picture of your bare ass in the art gallery where your mother is a volunteer and board member!

79

This Showcase Could Be Yours

Be a game show contestant.

Go on, girl, get that fifteen minutes of fame that's coming to you! Be a game show contestant and not only will you be able to brag about being on TV, you'll have a chance to score big prizes and go down in history with the words, "That's my final answer, Regis." At the very least, you'll score a lifetime supply of Rice-A-Roni, the San Francisco treat.

Play your cards right, and you could be the contestant standing between "Pat from Paducah, who enjoys gardening and needlepoint" and "Bob from Omaha, an insurance adjuster and proud father of twin boys." All you need to do is watch at the end of the show for details on how to become a contestant or member of the studio audience, and then write to the address on the screen for tickets and info.

If it's been a while since you watched game shows (that damn job really cuts down on the daytime TV!), here's a rundown of some of the longest standing game shows around.

"The Price Is Right"   Contestants guess the right price on all sorts of loot, from washer and dryer sets to stereo systems. The best contestants move on to the gripping Showcase Showdown and guess the correct cost of an entire showcase of stuff without going over the limit and blowing it all. Just remember: The Barbie-esque spokesmodels seem ageless, but brittle Bob Barker's gettin' a little "long in the tooth." Just be

> "Come on down!"
>
> —Rod Roddy, announcer for "The Price Is Right"

gentle with him when you run over to hug him and toss him in the air after winning that seven-day cruise to the Bahamas!

"Wheel of Fortune" Three contestants spin the gaudy, glittery wheel for the chance to solve word puzzles a chimpanzee could probably guess. The trick to winning is spinning the wheel so that it stops on big cash and prize items—and avoiding the "bust" slots, of course. To get psyched up, practice saying "Pat and Vanna, I would like to buy a vowel" with all the drama and gusto you can manage.

"Hollywood Squares" Contestants answer simple trivia questions for the chance to play a gigantic tic-tac-toe game, with a Hollywood star in each square. Judging from the B-list guest celebs that regularly appear, this show could easily be called "Hollywood Has-Beens," but if you're looking to rub elbows with Nipsey Russell and the guy who played Schneider on "One Day at a Time," this is the ticket!

"Jeopardy!" This game show appeals to the brainy TV crowd (an oxymoron?). Contestants are grilled on tough trivia questions read by consummate showhost Alex Trebek, who keeps the action moving and isn't afraid to blast the buzzer on contestants who dally when answering. If you know your seventeenth-century French literature and obscure world geography facts and aren't afraid of getting humiliated on national TV, "Jeopardy!" is for you.

 Ladies, Start Your Engines!

✳ Pay attention to the address and phone number given at the end of your favorite show for details on how to become a contestant.

✳ If you *really* want to be a game show contestant, register for several shows and reregister as often as allowed. Remember, you're competing against thousands of folks who are dying to meet Vanna and Pat!

✳ Almost all the coolest game shows have a website now. Log on for details and rules on how to become a contestant.

80

Empty Shelves Collect Nothing but Dust

Start collecting something you love.

If you're giddy about gilded wine goblets, crazy for cat's-eye shades, or loopy for leatherbound books, and you aren't afraid to spend the bucks to prove it, you're a collector. Collecting stuff can be a rewarding pastime as well as a way to own and enjoy more of whatever "objet d'art" floats your boat. Plus, being a collector of something pretty much guarantees that friends and relatives will know just the gift to get you for holidays and birthdays.

Do you hear the word *collection* and picture yourself in nerdy glasses and highwaters, poring over a dusty postage stamp album? Or perhaps you imagine buying Princess Di commemorative figurines out of *Good Housekeeping* magazine as you relax on your doily-armed couch, dressed in rollers and a polyester housecoat. Forget the figurines, forgo the postage stamps—although those Elvis ones are pretty cool. These days, people collect all sorts of cool stuff and are limited only by imagination and budget. Antique toys, shot glasses, matchbook covers, and old 45s are all fun and funky items to acquire. Sorry, collecting phone numbers from the bar doesn't really count.

The boons of collecting? The very fact that you collect something implies that you must continue hunting and grabbing up stuff to add to your collection. After all, when it comes to collecting, the more the merrier. That's why they call it collecting! As a "collector" you

169

> **"You're only as old as your comic collection."**
>
> –Dan Thorsland

are officially no longer an indiscriminate buyer of needless crap. ("As a matter of fact, I *don't* have enough candle holders!") When friends accuse you of being a shopaholic, squelch their accusations by proclaiming yourself an avid collector, so that your fervent spending is elevated to a dignified pursuit. ("I am not a shameless shoe hound, I'm a stiletto collector!")

Collections make a unique addition to your home and provide a no-fail conversation piece. It's as simple as picking up more of whatever it is you like and finding a creative way to display them. Love old Liberace recordings? Next time you're wandering around the flea market, keep your eyes peeled for eight-tracks and records featuring the flamboyant pianist. Crazy about tiny Buddha carvings? Start collecting a variety of them and have a shelf full of The Enlightened One! If good luck truly comes from rubbing his belly, rubbing all the bellies in your Buddha collection must make for a truly charmed existence.

One final thought: You might want to put that collection of Play-girls and funky novelty bongs somewhere besides your living room bookshelf when Grandma comes over for dinner.

 Ladies, Start Your Engines!

✳ You name the collection, there's a website for it. Search the Internet to meet other folks who share your passion for stamps or Barbies or old sewing machines.

✳ Consider keeping a list of all the items in your collection, just in case anything of value is ever lost or stolen.

✳ Anything worth collecting is worth preserving. Protect your collection in a lined box, a keepsake album, or a dustproof glass case.

81

A Potent and Poisonous Potion

Try your hand at alchemy and mix your own perfume.

Perfume is useful for a lot more than just spritzing your armpits when you wake up late and can't take a shower! Most women don't consider perfume an absolute necessity—except perhaps the frilly, high-maintenance-type chick who won't leave home without her lipliner and owns a wardrobe that could dress the population of Cleveland—but that's really too bad. Scent can lift your spirits and be a signature of your unique personality.

While all of our personalities are unique, the perfumes regularly available on the market are not. Perfume is like fashion—one hits the market and becomes the hot fragrance that everybody's gotta have, and soon every Jane, Doris, and Sally is walking around smelling identical. Not a big deal, unless the following scenario has happened to you:

Friday night. Hot date with New Boyfriend is scheduled for eight o'clock. You dress to the nines and spritz on the Latest Hot Fragrance in giddy anticipation. You show up at the swanky restaurant and hug New Boyfriend hello, only to notice a puzzled and disconcerted look on his face. After asking New Boyfriend what's wrong, he awkwardly explains that the Latest Hot Fragrance you're wearing is a painful reminder of his longtime love and latest Ex-Girlfriend, who always wore Latest

> "To attract men, I wear a perfume called New Car Interior."
>
> —Rita Rudner

Hot Fragrance, and even used to spray it on his pillow. You suffer through the main course in smelly silence. By the time dessert arrives, you are cursing the day you ever smelled, much less bought, Latest Hot Fragrance and promptly pour it down the sink when you get home from your date, which ended early. New Boyfriend went home without accepting your invitation for a nightcap. He probably ran home to sniff his pillow in memory of Ex-Girlfriend!

Maybe that's an exaggeration, but this worst-case scenario can be avoided by mixing and wearing custom perfume! It can be as simple as mixing two scents together to smell the fabulous result. This can be lots of fun if you have perfumes you don't care for but don't want to toss. Be careful, though, you could unwittingly end up smelling like Renuzit room deodorizer!

If you don't want to chance it, order a custom-made perfume. Several companies custom blend perfumes to reflect the wearer's personality. With most companies, you design the fragrance by selecting personality traits and the perfumer "translates" your picks into a corresponding fragrance element. For example, rose equals romantic, citrus scents equal energetic. When these various scents are blended, a perfume is created that's as unique as the wearer.

And next time New Boyfriend asks what perfume you're wearing, just bat your eyelashes and gush innocently, "I'm not wearing any! I just naturally smell this good!"

 Ladies, Start Your Engines!

✳ If you're going for a scent that says "mysterious," choose lotus blossom. If you're more of a natural beauty, choose magnolia scents. To convey drama, choose scents with spicy undertones.

✳ Perfume Oils by Maisha sells custom blended oils. These are great because they contain no alcohol and can also be used as a bath oil. Check out www.wesmellgood.com for prices and products.

✳ Read *Perfumes, Splashes & Colognes: Discovering and Crafting Your Personal Fragrances* by Nancy Booth or one of the many aromatherapy books on the shelves.

82

Spooky Sorceress and Witchy Woman

Visit a psychic.

Have you lived another life before? Is there a tall, dark stranger in your
future? How do you put a hex on your ex? Visit a psychic, and you can
discover the answers to these and many other burning questions of the
universe.

If the word *psychic* conjures a picture of a gypsy woman with oversize gold earrings, spangles, and a phony Transylvanian accent, think
again. Not all psychics are phony, carnival sideshow entertainment.
Some feel they have a true gift for sensing the future, and plenty of
people swear by them! Even so, sometimes psychics are as much for
the novelty of the experience as they are for revealing future events.

If you want more bang for your buck and truly enjoy the levitating
experience, skip the LaToya Jackson 900 number and visit an actual
psychic. When you go to a psychic in person, you'll get the full experience of sitting at a rickety folding table, inhaling a cloud of potent
incense as your psychic gives a reading, brows furrowed in cosmic
concentration while flipping down tarot cards. The best you can expect
with a 900 number is a gum-cracking waitress who's answering the
phone in between shifts and talking extra
S-L-O-W to burn up the precious and
pricey phone minutes.

Psychics do their work using a variety
of methods—tarot cards, rune stones,
looking into your palm, or simply
"sensing your energy." Keep in mind

> "Here's something to think
> about: How come you never
> see a headline like 'Psychic
> Wins Lottery'?"
> —Jay Leno

that, except for perhaps a few charlatans, psychics truly believe they have the gift of clairvoyance, though they aren't right 100 percent of the time. They are *not* snake oil salesmen in silk scarves. If you're skeptical of someone's psychic ability, it's polite to bite your tongue and sit through the reading for the fun of it, rather than fire annoying questions trying to make the psychic "prove" his or her ability: "OK, what am I thinking now?" "What's my middle name?" Remember, nobody bursts into your cubicle demanding that you justify *your* skills, right? You can always check references and credentials beforehand if you're that uptight about being ripped off.

Finding a psychic is not as hard as you think and even small towns usually have at least one soothsayer. If there's a New Age bookstore in town, call to find out if there's a psychic who works out of the store. Or look in the phone book under *psychic* and see what's listed. Big fans of the psychic experience will tell you to avoid going to roadside fortune tellers that advertise with big neon signs reading "Palm Reading Here—$10." After all, the most successful and effective fortune tellers are booked through word of mouth and references alone, not big advertisements.

If you'd rather do the soothsaying yourself, pick up a deck of tarot cards and take a peek into your own future. Most decks come with a short instruction book to guide tarot rookies through the basic meanings behind each card. Invite friends and family over and offer to perform a tarot reading on them. Wearing a jewel-encrusted turban is optional.

 Ladies, Start Your Engines!

✳ Check the Personal Services section of the classified ads for psychic listings.

✳ Lots of radio stations host psychic call-in shows periodically, so tune in.

✳ Want to develop your own psychic ability? Pick up *Are You Psychic?: Unlocking the Power Within* by Hans Holzer or *Be Psychic Now!* by Nathaniel Friedland.

83

Soled, Stiletto, and Strappy

Design your own shoes.

From strappy little sandals to patent leather boots, we've all got a pair of shoes that we just love! Whether you're a froufrou chick with a closet solely for soles, or a basics kind of woman with a few select styles, nothin' beats a cool pair of shoes! It doesn't matter whether you are stepping up the career ladder, stepping onto the dance floor, or stepping out with a hunky honey, footwear is fundamental.

Unfortunately, cool shoes (I mean *really* cool shoes—the kind that make other people say, "Hey, I love your shoes!") are hard to come by. Comb through your average Kinney's, Bakers, or other mall shoe store, and you are presented with two basic choices: cheap, too-trendy platforms that leave you tottering atop four-inch vinyl heels or bland patent leather pumps for work that make you look like every other Corporate Connie in town.

Step into a department store shoe section and your choices can be equally dismal, though more expensive. It's the same platform boots for club hopping and sensible pumps for desk jockeys, only with better vinyl and a bigger selection of patent leather colors.

And if you think you're gonna march right down to a downtown shoe boutique for frisky footwear that would make Imelda Marcos drool, forget it—unless you're willing to forgo paying that pesky rent and Visa bill for the month! We love leopard-print Prada boots as much as

175

> "If the shoe fits, it's too expensive."
> —Adrienne Gusoff

the next girl, but let's be realistic—the only way you're gonna own a closet full of shoes *that* cool is to find yourself a sugar daddy!

Here's an idea—design the shoes yourself! If you have an idea for a cool pair of shoes, just sketch out your idea and take it to a cobbler, who will make the shoes of your dreams. Shoes custom made and designed for you . . . it's like a sole fantasy come true, a vision in leather and laces! Plus, you'll be helping support the work of a cobbler, practically a lost art in these days of mass-produced shoes. Check the phone book under *shoe repair* for shoe shops that employ cobblers, and call around for prices and details on making custom-designed shoes.

Can't find a cobbler or just want the next best thing? Take some old shoes to a shoe repairer and have a funky new sole put on! Adding a new sole is a great way to update a pair of boots that you love but that have a '70s-style stacked heel you love to hate.

 Ladies, Start Your Engines!

✳ Pick up the books *Make Your Own Shoes* by Mary Wales Loomis or *Paper Shoe Book: Everything You Need to Know to Make Your Own Paper Shoes* by Julian Horsey and Chris Knowles.

✳ If your cobbler can't customize your shoes from the sole up, ask what it costs to dye them instead.

✳ Take your custom-shoe hunt on-line with www.thoseshoes.com or www.digitoe.com.

84

Silly Solo Sorority Sisters

Pull a panty raid on yourself and purge those ratty, old-lady undies for good.

OK, ladies, be honest—how many times have you rummaged through your lingerie drawer in search of something scanty and saucy to find that the only panties you have are a snagged and dingy pair of cotton briefs big enough to sail a ship? Even if no one else has to look at you in your Skivvies, you have to look at yourself! Toss those old panties out and opt for something that doesn't look like it was purchased from the buck bin at a blue light special, back when there were blue light specials!

Sure, every girl—except for glitzy high-maintenance types, of course—has a tendency to get a little sloppy with the Skivvies. (Hey, it's not like you wear 'em out where the world will see 'em!) But, like Mom always said, you never know when you might get in an accident on the way to work. You certainly don't want those hunky fire and rescue workers who have to cut your pants off to find panties your grandma wouldn't be caught dead in! Why don undies that make you look like Tillie, the slovenly washer woman with a gigantic mole on her face, when you can feel like Zakistra, the mysterious chick who zips around town in an exotic sports car? Women named Zakistra don't wear tattered white briefs that come up to their armpits!

Roll up your sleeves, pull out your undie drawer, and toss out anything that matches the following descriptions:

> "A lady is one who never shows her underwear unintentionally."
> —Lillian Day

* Anything with kitties, Disney characters, or cartoon stuff on it (You are too old to dress like you're going to a junior high slumber party)
* Anything with elastic that has long since stopped elasticizing
* Anything stained (gross!) or otherwise discolored, including whities washed with a few too many red shirts

Toss them for good. Don't stash them in the back as the "all my cute panties are in the laundry" stash—because if they've lasted since high school (amazing they still fit!), then they are tough enough to fight their way back to the front of the lingerie drawer!

Once you've cleaned house, you can strut around in style wearing a micromini like Sharon Stone in *Basic Instinct* and give complete strangers random crotch shots. One warning, though: All that open air gets cold. God created panties for a reason, not just to keep Victoria's Secret rolling in dough or for broads to sell to incarcerated men for a tidy profit—or for sly chicks to leave behind in their boyfriend's apartment to mark their territory.

When you replenish your panty pantry, indulge in choices ranging from cheap and comfy cotton standbys to outrageously daring and crotchless, edible or otherwise, designed to raise a few . . . um . . . eyebrows.

 Ladies, Start Your Engines!

* Panties have strange sizes, with size 7 being "large." If you don't know your size, ask a clerk to explain the sizes to you.

* Be sure to throw some practical pairs in with your lacy choices—you want them to look fabulous, but you want to be comfortable too!

* Buy quality stuff, even if you're a cheap chick. There's nothing worse than having new panties fall apart after two washings.

85

Chicks Chug Beer Too

Discover the pleasures of home brewing.

Nothing beats the pleasure of pouring yourself a cold one after a long hard week. Beer is the sudsy, yeasty treat that unites the masses. However, after paying a pretty penny for beer, you're gonna need a drink. Gone are the days when you sallied up to the bar, ordered a plain old Miller, and paid a buck or two for it. In these gourmet microbrew times, you gotta know your Bocks from your Bitters, your Pilsners from your Hefeweissen, and you'll pay about as much as you would for a 1974 Corbieres Merlot. In addition, there's always the risk of ordering something you've never heard of and paying nine dollars to be served something similar to the pisswater you chugged in high school for maximum buzz.

The way around this discouraging dilemma is to brew your own beer! The good thing about home brewing is that learning about it mostly involves drinking, and you already know how to do that. You can brew your own to mimic a brand you already know and love, or you can try making something totally new, all at less than half the cost of buying beer from a liquor store. Just think—all the money you'll save by home brewing can be applied to a quality rehab center later!

Consider the possibilities of becoming a beer hound: You can throw wild-woman beer bashes (kind of like frat parties but with just your girlfriends and nobody peeing off the balcony!). If you're having trouble

> "Beer. Now there's a temporary solution."
> —Homer Simpson

meeting new people, just mention free beer! And this is your perfect excuse to add some bar paraphernalia to your tastefully appointed living room furnishings—just slap up a couple of Coors Light bikini posters, a neon Old Milwaukee sign, and wood paneling. And don't forget the pool table!

Since most recipes require that you make a monster-size batch, you might find yourself literally swimming in beer. Ever had a fantasy of sitting in a tub filled with golden, sudsy beer? Now's your chance! If the beer's good, you'll be stocked for a long, long time, unless you make a habit of dating entire fraternity houses! If it's undrinkable, the worst that will happen is a bad case of the beer farts, and enough left over to make homemade beer shampoo for a year.

Ready to become a beer-brewing babe? It helps if you have a collection of old bottles (not a problem for recyclers) and a big jar to mix and ferment the beer in for a few weeks. Plus, you need the ingredients, which include water, yeast, hops, and malt. A cool, dark basement for fermentation comes in handy, too. Plenty of places already sell beer-brewing kits for around fifty dollars. (They can be purchased over the Internet.) If you like lots of free advice, visit a beer- or wine-making store. Not only will they have all the supplies you need, but you'll more than likely be helped by a charming overly enthusiastic hippy type who has perfected his brewing techniques in the sink in a VW van.

Just remember—you've had too much beer if you go for a routine physical and the nurse announces your urine sample is a golden amber and has a head on it.

 Ladies, Start Your Engines!

✳ It goes without saying that if you're knocking back beers, don't get behind the wheel of a car. Calling a taxi is way cheaper than fighting a DUI charge.

✳ If you're throwing a beer bash, play "Spin the Bottle" with your friends—for old-times' sake.

✳ Check out www.homebrew.com for the latest in brewing tips and resources.

86

Stroll Down Memory Lane

Create a memory wall.

Ah, memories. . . . We all have fond recollections of days gone by, whether it's of romping with dearly departed Ms. Kittykins, hanging out with a hunky ex-beau (before you started referring to him simply as "that jerk"), or the way your size-8 butt looked before it swallowed a whole ham and ballooned into a size 14.

Chances are you've got photos of such blissful days packed away in some musty desk drawer, next to a dried-up bottle of nail polish, expired dry cleaning coupons, and assorted spare earring backs. Is that any way to treat the only evidence you have of these fond memories? Do something constructive while you pine away for the past. Dig those old photos out and put them on display, creating a funky "memory wall" scene for a stroll down memory lane.

A memory wall-hanging doesn't mean just sticking snapshots up on a wall and calling it good. Glue lots of different objects to your wall-hanging and scribble little notes and thoughts for a unique multimedia display that's grade school diorama cool! All it takes is a big chunk of canvas or poster board, a good imagination, and a truckload of glue. Here are a few ideas to get you started:

* Took a fun trip with a pal recently? Dig out those crazy snapshots and glue them on with Modge Podge or a glue gun. Next to each pic write a caption like "Check out our

> "These childhood memories—I have them often but can usually keep them under control with the use of drugs."
>
> —Dave Barry

shades!" or "Here we are in Las Vegas . . . or rather Lost Wages" with a bold pen or marker. Glue up any postcards, flyers, or playbills you picked up along the way too. You can even glue up that too-bare string bikini you wore to remind you of when the top came flying off and floated to the shallow end just after your spectacular dive!

* Reminiscing about your younger, thinner days? Dig out those shots that show off your previously slender self and glue them on a big canvas sheet posted right next to the fridge, along with your Welcome to Weight Watchers brochures! And those "skinny pants" you've been saving since 1992 for inspiration? Dig 'em out of the back of your closet and glue them right up there!

* Rather than a memory wall, create a fantasy wall of something you hope for the future! Have your eye on a hot new convertible down at the car dealership? The only thing standing in the way of you and your dream machine is a set of car keys—and forty thousand bucks. Put up shots of your star car from *Car and Driver* magazine, and you'll be picturing yourself cruising along Highway 101 in no time!

 Ladies, Start Your Engines!

* Invest in a glue gun. They're cheap, and they work like a charm on projects like this!

* For extra pizzazz, start with colored poster board rather than boring white.

* If you're mounting heavy stuff such as coins to your wall-hanging, glue them near the center so they won't weigh down the finished piece and make it hang lopsided.

87

Invest in Yourself

Join an investment club and increase your fiscal fitness.

They say it's not the money you make but the money you keep that separates the money moguls from the paupers. If your idea of saving money is throwing all your spare change in a jar on your dresser, take note: The sooner you start saving some real cash, the sooner you'll be able to reap the rewards of being financially savvy (not bouncing checks would be great, too). Join an investment club and you'll be rolling in dough in no time!

Why should you care to invest your money? There are plenty of reasons to start saving! For one thing, some of the coolest stuff life has to offer comes with a hefty price tag. Sure the best things in life—love, family, all that stuff—are free, but houses and cars cost a pretty penny. Then there's retirement to worry about—saving money today means you won't have to live in a rickety trailer eating dog food when you're an old woman!

How do investment clubs work? It's much like any other membership club, but the goal here is to educate members on financial matters, as well as to pool investment funds. Each member pays an initiation fee and a monthly fee, which goes into the community pot and is then invested. Clubs usually meet monthly or bimonthly to decide where to invest

> "From birth to 18 a girl needs good parents. From 18 to 35, she needs good looks. From 35 to 55, good personality. From 55 on, she needs good cash. I'm saving my money."
> —Sophie Tucker

their chunk of change, talk stock tips, and dish the dirt about mutual funds, retirement planning, and other money matters. Since your money is being combined with that of other members, it's best to think of an investment club as a long-term commitment. Each club has its own unique set of rules regarding departing members and how they collect their piece of the pie when they depart.

The financial advice you pick up in such a club can be invaluable. Hanging around financial whizzes in the know can only be a good thing. Just think, if only you'd bought stock in the company that manufactures Viagra before it really took off . . .

  ### Ladies, Start Your Engines!

❋ Contact the AAII, or American Association of Individual Investors, for education and investment resources on the stock market, mutual funds, and retirement planning. Visit them on the Web at www.aaii.com.

❋ Next time you're looking for something to watch on TV, check out CNBC's "Moneyline," CNN's "Wall Street Week," or Fox News Channel's "Fox on Money."

❋ Read the book *One Up on Wall Street*, by Peter Lynch with John Rothchild, written by an investment whiz who describes things the average investor can do to make more money.

❋ Also check out Beth Kobliner's book *Get a Financial Life: Personal Finances in Your 20s and 30s*. It's wonderfully accessible and comprehensive.

88

Dream a Little Dream with Me

Learn to interpret your dreams.

Picture this: You're stranded on a desert island, and you're wearing your prom dress. Suddenly, out of the jungle bursts a wild animal, some sort of cross between a rhino and a poodle . . . only it has pink fur. You panic and start to run. All of a sudden you're at the beach when an '89 Honda floats up from out of nowhere, with fins instead of wheels. You get in the car and drive/float away to escape the pink rhino-poodle, and the radio's playing your favorite song, except all the words are sung in Portuguese.

Welcome to the crazy world of dreams, where your unconscious mind runs wild and free while the rest of you tries to get some sleep. Dreams might just be figments of the imagination, but the emotions they bring forth can be very real. That's why dreams make such a lasting impression on us. Remember the terror you felt when you woke up in a cold sweat after a nightmare? Or the joy of dreaming that you won the lottery? Or the bliss you felt after dreaming you were hot tubbing with Tom Cruise?

Ask any expert and they'll each have a different theory about what dreams are and why we have them. But most agree that dreams have a deeper purpose than simply entertaining us or giving us something to talk about in the morning. Learn how to interpret your dreams, and you

> "Dreams do not deceive, they do not lie, they do not distort or misguide. They are invariably seeking to express something that the ego does not know and does not understand."
>
> —Carl Jung

just might be able to better understand what your own subconscious is telling you.

If you're new to dream interpretation, you could be a little intimidated by the millions of theories on everything from allegorical dreams to deciphering premonitions to lucid dreaming to psychoanalytic gibberish. Check out lots of different schools of thought so that you can choose the ideas that make the most sense to you. And remember: You are the authority when it comes to interpreting your dreams. Dreaming of an apple orchard may not mean much to most folks, but if you lived next to an orchard growing up, you might be unconsciously longing for those carefree days you spent as a kid.

Here are a few common dream symbols—they are out of context, so take these with a grain of salt.

> *Bridge*: To dream of crossing a bridge represents overcoming difficulties.
>
> *Old house*: To dream of a house you used to live in means you'll soon have good news to rejoice over.
>
> *Hair*: If you dream of your hair turning gray or falling out, you're due to experience trouble or disappointment (no surprise there).
>
> *Drowning*: If you dream you're drowning it means you feel overwhelmed in your life.
>
> *Lucky*: To dream you are lucky when you're feeling down means prosperity is coming and that your wishes will come true.
>
> *Pregnant*: If you dream you're pregnant when you are actually pregnant, it foretells of a safe delivery. If you're not pregnant . . . better get that birth control prescription refilled!

 Ladies, Start Your Engines!

❋ Pick up a copy of *The Complete Idiot's Guide to Interpreting Your Dreams* by Marci Pliskin or *Dream Dictionary: A Guide to Dreams and Sleep Experiences* by Tony Crisp.

❋ Keep paper and pen by your bed so you can record dreams when you wake up.

❋ Learn more on-line by visiting www.dreamemporium.com or www.templeofdreams.com.

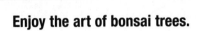
Your Own Japanese Garden

Enjoy the art of bonsai trees.

If you're into hobbies that offer instant gratification, skip ahead— the art of bonsai, or cultivating dwarf trees, can take years, even decades, to master. Maybe that's because bonsai was developed in Japan one thousand years ago, before microwave ovens, automated teller machines, and instant messaging shortened everyone's attention span.

Bonsai can be a beautiful and rewarding way to appreciate nature. In bonsai cultivation, the plants are kept small and in proportion to their natural models by growing them in small containers and pruning and forming branches to the desired shape by training them with wire coils. The idea of bonsai is to re-create the ravages of nature on trees on a reduced scale by simulating natural and environmental conditions such as age, extreme weather, and the twisting power of the wind.

If this all sounds a little too studious to you, here are some great reasons to be a budding bonsai fan:

* Re-creating the effects of nature and imposing your will upon a helpless tree satisfies your God complex.
* Bonsai trees lend an air of Eastern mystique to your decor, without costing you $500 like the oriental screen you saw at that funky antique store.

> "Solitary trees, if they grow at all, grow strong."
> —Sir Winston Churchill

* If you want to impress your Japanese date, bonsai is better than attempting to prepare sushi and risking a potential food-poisoning incident.
* It's less commitment than a pet, and you won't feel as crappy if your tree dies.

Your journey into the world of bonsai needn't be too expensive. Once you buy your starter plant and supplies, you're pretty much set. Experts recommend starting with a dwarf juniper, but your local garden center may carry other options. You'll also need some basic tools, including pruning shears and wire to "train" the branches.

You might also want to pick up a basic bonsai book to tell you how to get started and to guide you through pruning and watering techniques, since wise advice on bonsai can be hard to find at the Kmart Garden Center down the street. It's doubtful (though possible) that some seventeen-year-old cashier with pink hair and a spike through his tongue will want to converse with you at length on expert pruning techniques and bonsai's contribution to Japanese culture.

 Ladies, Start Your Engines!

* Check out these books for bonsai basics:
    * *Bonsai* and *101 Essential Tips: Bonsai* by Harry Tomlinson
    * *The Bonsai Survival Manual Tree-by-Tree Guide* by Colin Lewis
    * *Beginning Bonsai: The Gentle Art of Miniature Tree Growing* by Shirley and Larry Student

* For information about bonsai and clubs in your area, check out the American Bonsai Society's website at www.absbonsai.org, or check out www.bonsaiweb.com for tons of tips, links, software, and supplies.

* Ask your local specialty gardening center if they offer one-day classes on bonsai.

90

YourNameHere.com

When you think of the Internet, what comes to mind? Horny teenagers downloading Pamela Anderson nudie shots before their parents get home? Bill Gates's continued campaign for world domination? Freakishly ugly guys logging on as "TanStud69" in hope of getting cyberlaid in a chat room?

Well, the Web isn't just for techie geeks anymore. It's for everyone—and that includes you! So, why not hang up your own little shingle along the information superhighway by creating a personal website? It's easier than you think, and chances are you can do it for free through your Internet service provider.

Why a personal website? It's a great way to keep in touch with friends and family and pass along news, fave recipes, and links to other sites you love. Got pictures of yourself romping at the beach with your new puppy? Post them on your website so everyone can ooh and aah over little Rover. Are you the singer babe in an all-girl punk band? Post your playing schedule on-line, so your legions of fans will know to catch your act at the Punk Palace. Planning a party? Post directions to your house, along with a few surprise hints to titillate your guests, such as "Costume party: Dress as your favorite '6os rock star" or "Don't miss the karaoke showdown at midnight."

A personal website can also come in handy during the job hunt. Post your

> "The 'Net is a waste of time, and that's exactly what's right about it."
>
> —William Gibson

resume, including a list of professional accomplishments, on your website. Then shamelessly give your Web address out to everyone you come across during the job hunt. Think of it as a way to look professional and high-tech without having to post your resume on one of those job-hunting sites. That way if your boss is snooping around on Monster.com, she won't happen upon your recently posted resume.

Depending on your Internet service provider, you could be entitled to a free personal website as a membership perk. AOL offers members a free site and provides the downloadable software you need to create your pages. Or, if you want a bigger and more sophisticated site than what's available for free, pick up a Web design software package such as Microsoft Front Page and let your creativity run wild. If you need help finding an Internet company to put your website files on-line and host it for you, check the phone book under *Internet Services,* and you're sure to find a million companies to choose from, many of which would be happy to design a website for you. Just pick a cool domain name, and you're all set! But, just so you know, "she's-all-that-and-a-bag-of-chips.com" and "cyberbabe.com" are already taken.

 Ladies, Start Your Engines!

✳ Even if your website's not ready for prime time, reserve the domain name before someone else does at www.register.com.

✳ Visit your local software store for scads of products that will make designing your website as easy as pie.

✳ Check out other personal websites first to get ideas for the graphic styles and content you like best.

91

'40s Femmes in Funky Fedoras

Start watching old movies and let ladies like Bette Davis, Katharine Hepburn, and Lauren Bacall teach you how to be a vintage vixen.

In the Hollywood movies of the '30s and '40s, women didn't leave the house without mink stoles. With engraved cigarette cases and outrageously ornate evening gowns, these dames looked cool and had attitude to spare. Forget fake boobs, bony asses, and silicone lip injections—actresses of yesteryear knew how to work a room and reign as queens of the cocktail lounge with just witty banter and big, batty lashes.

Vintage Hollywood flicks still seem so fresh and original today because they were conceived before the movie industry had a chance to rehash every story line into pulverized mush. Any movie that doesn't involve aliens, spaceships, good cops gone bad, or Sylvester Stallone can't be too bad! It's refreshing to watch a woman protagonist that doesn't feel compelled to diet down to a whopping ninety-pound size 2 before appearing on screen.

Even if you don't get a kick out of the '40s femmes, old movies are worth it for the male characters as well. These tough guys preceded the days when Brad Pitt and company came on the scene with their little girlyman bodies and frosted hair. They were cool in a gentlemanly, vintage-suit-with-spitshined-shoes sort of way. Who wouldn't rather watch Clark Gable or Cary Grant woo a dame without messing up a single Brylcreemed hair than endure

191

> "The face of Garbo is an Idea, that of Hepburn an Event."
> —Roland Barthes

watching an overpaid Bruce Willis ape his way through a love scene? And who wouldn't want to be the chick pinned under Burt Lancaster in the makeout scene on the beach in *From Here to Eternity*? Most women would get sand in their Skivvies any day of the week for five minutes pinned under a landslide of Lancaster!

By now you're saying, "All the chicks in those old movies were the fawning, simpering, housewifey types. They were a decade behind June Cleaver!" But that's where you're wrong. There are plenty of modern female characters to be found in old movies, swaggering chicks with guts and gusto who kicked ass first and took names later—some are so tough they put women's roles from modern movies to shame.

 Ladies, Start Your Engines!

Here are a few flicks to get you started:

✳ *The Bigamist:* A salesman secretly marries both a wealthy woman from an uppity L.A. family and a waitress in a Chinese restaurant. This quirky movie is directed by and stars B-movie queen Ida Lupino, along with her real-life ex-husband.

✳ *Johnny Guitar:* Joan Crawford plays a tough saloon owner on the dusty plains, fighting off enemies tooth and nail. She swaggers around in too-tight chaps and slams whiskey with the gunslingers. Nobody screws with Joan in this flick!

✳ *All About Eve:* The classic 1950 flick in which Bette Davis plays a grand dame of theater bumped from the throne by a scheming, seemingly innocent underling. The claws come out as the two plot to outfox each other. Featuring lots of dry martinis and the timeless quip: "Fasten your seat belts—it's going to be a bumpy night."

92

Move Over, Clapton!

Learn to play guitar.

Whether you're a fan of smooth, strummy, mellow ballads or hard-rockin' heavy metal, everyone on the planet seems to like guitar music. And if you think listening to music is fun, playing music is even more of a kick! You don't need to learn to read music to start playing—plenty of professional guitarists wouldn't know a treble clef if it bit 'em on the ass!

It's not just pimply teenage geeks who are learning to play guitar, with visions of MTV videos dancing in their head. Great women guitarists abound; let the likes of Bonnie Raitt, Melissa Etheridge, and Courtney Love inspire you. The guitar is perfectly suited for neophyte and virtuoso players alike. You can learn just enough chords to strum along with the radio, or master your "chops" and learn to play lightning-fast electric solos. You could be starting your own chick band in no time! All you need is a decent ear for music, a little patience, and a bit of finger dexterity and you're in business.

So you're ready to start jamming on the guitar, but you don't know where to start? First, decide what type of music you'd like to play. Feel like learning slow, strummy ballads and down-home country tunes? Or maybe some gritty, funky blues tunes? What you need is an acoustic guitar, the mellow-sounding wood-bodied instrument played without amplifiers or electronic effects for that "unplugged" tone.

> "You're talking to someone who really understands rock music."
>
> —Tipper Gore

Remember the kind of guitar Elvis would pull out of nowhere in the movie *Clambake*, when he was fixin' to swoon a giggly blonde or liven up the beach party? That's an acoustic guitar.

Acoustics abound at junk stores, yard sales, and pawnshops everywhere, with decent ones starting at about a hundred bucks. The better deal, though, is to drop into your local music store and rent one—and inquire about lessons while you're at it. Not only will you learn on a decent instrument, you'll minimize the investment made on a hobby that just might have a short shelf life. After all, not everyone wants a hobby that involves developing calluses on fingertips!

If you're more of a rocker chick, rent an electric guitar. True, more equipment goes with an electric guitar. Things like amplifiers, electronic effects, and cords, just to name a few. But plug it all in, learn a few notes, and start jamming, and you'll swear you are Jimi Hendrix reincarnated! Besides, when you're feeding a video vixen fantasy of being the front chick of a rock band, strumming away on some wimpy acoustic just won't cut it! Again, your local music store rents everything you need to get started.

 Ladies, Start Your Engines!

✳ Check out www.guitarists.net for resources like instruction, sheet music, chat rooms, retailers—basically everything you want to know about the guitar.

✳ Visit *How to Play Guitar* Online at www.howguitar.com. This guitar magazine includes one hour of audio lessons on CD with every issue.

✳ Plenty of guitar teachers advertise in the music want ads of the local paper. Some even offer a free first lesson!

93

Playing Polynesian Princess

Take up hula dancing.

If you've ever been to the Hawaiian islands, you've probably seen hula dance performed and admired the grass-skirted beauties' fluid movements. Maybe you've even been pulled from your seat into the sand to move along with the dancers. You're game for practically anything after a couple of mai tais!

Hula dance, more than a tourist-trap novelty, has a history reaching far beyond the typical Honolulu Holiday Inn setting. A little hula history for you: Originally a sacred dance, hula was performed by select dancers who were taught the movements by temple priests. The dancers' fluid hand and swaying hip movements expressed themes of life and death, as well as love for the beauty of the islands and devotion to the Polynesian gods. Uptight missionaries who arrived in Hawaii in the 1820s banned the dance as suggestive, but a wise King Kalakaua defied the ban in the 1870s and even established hula schools.

Thanks to King K., hula is thriving today, just waiting for you to try it! Even if you don't have a single ounce of Polynesian blood in you, you'll be able to master some basic hip movements and learn the hand gestures by taking a few simple classes. Check with dance schools in your area to see who offers hula classes. Chances are some of the larger studios have some sort of class scheduled, even if it's only a related form of dance, like Tahitian dance.

> "Mai hilahila!"
> —Hawaiian for
> "Don't be bashful!"

195

Adult education centers sometimes offer classes like these, with a six-week stint to give you a taste of the dance.

The best part about hula classes is the kick you get out of watching others try it! Do you feel fat in a leotard and intimidated by the idea of stomping your way through dance moves, surrounded by snotty, graceful women? Sign up anyway—you will be surprised and comforted when you arrive to find the dance studio filled with spunky, chunky housewives in their fifties who let their grass skirts fly and don't give a damn what anybody thinks! Besides, the hula's accompanying ukelele music is always better when you hear it with a group. Your studio may even provide fake grass skirts you can wear for class.

Can't find a class that suits you or live where no classes are offered? No problem. You can purchase instructional videos that will teach you how to hula in the privacy of your own home! Those of you who are "rhythmically challenged" won't feel awkward trying to master the movements with only your cat around to witness it. Plus, the uninhibited can really get into it: Fashion a bra out of two coconut halves and some twine and you're ready to roll! Stick with it and you'll be mastering the movements of the island dance faster than you can say "Don Ho"!

 Ladies, Start Your Engines!

✳ You can buy hula videos from the video section at www. booklines.com.

✳ If you'd rather skip the class and just shake your hips to hula music, pick up the albums *Hukilau Hulas* and *Hawaiian Hula Chants and Songs.*

✳ If you're planning on making a coconut bra, buy a prescored coconut from the store. They split evenly to make two perfect halves!

94

Is That a Roll of Quarters in Your Pocket or Is It Trompe l'Oeil?

Finesse the fine art of illusion with trompe l'oeil.

Tour any decorating showcase, go to any parade of homes, or pick up any decorating mag lately, and you'll see *trompe l'oeil*, or "fool the eye," painting. Trompe l'oeil is the French painting technique that is hot, hot, hot! This hard-to-master style of painting landscapes and objects with realistic detail can turn a blank wall into a rolling Italian landscape or a yucky plain panel into a flowery, forested garden gazebo.

The best trompe l'oeil creates visions so realistic that viewers have to look twice to realize the object is a painting and not real. A sunny windowsill painted directly on drywall will have you trying to lean out to catch a summer breeze. The possibilities for beautiful paintings are endless, limited only by your imagination and artistic ability.

How convincing "fool the eye" artwork is depends on the talent of the person doing the "tromping." If you're pretty handy with a paintbrush and think you can create the impression of rolling tundra, why not take a stab at it? The worst that can happen is that after dropping a hundred bucks on an arsenal of paint and dedicating a few frustrating afternoons, your "fool the eye" painting looks just plain foolish. So paint over it!

Not everyone aced high school art class. If you take a step back and discover your sweeping mountain vista looks more like a can of green paint exploded onto your living room wall, you'll know

> "A man paints with his brain and not with his hands."
> —Michelangelo

it's time to hire an artist who specializes in trompe l'oeil to paint for you. You can find an artist by asking around at art supply stores or art colleges. Better yet, any decorating showcase or model home featuring trompe l'oeil is sure to have a fat stack of the artist's business cards for prospective clients. Checking out the showcase is also a good way to see what kind of form and technique the artist uses before you blow a bundle on your own trompe l'oeil.

Struggling to choose a scene that you want eternally emblazoned on your bedroom wall? You could take a cue from designer books and do the typical gazebo-with-fruit-orchard-in-the-background scene, but with a little creativity, surely you can think of something you'd *really* like to look at! May we suggest

* Brendan Fraser
* A glittering starscape on a midnight blue backdrop, complete with constellations and planets
* Brendan Fraser, sweaty and shirtless
* A surreal ocean scene, surrounded by tropical fish and sea creatures
* Brendan Fraser, sweaty and shirtless in too-tight leather pants

 Ladies, Start Your Engines!

* If you like a trompe l'oeil scene in a decorating magazine, clip it or copy it so you can use it as a model for your own walls.

* If it's your first time using such a daring decorating technique, choose a simple design such as clouds against a blue sky.

* Check with some of the art supply stores or home decorating shops in town. Some offer one-day classes in painting techniques such as trompe l'oeil.

95

Reading, Writing, and Ranting

Spout your personal views by starting a 'zine or newsletter.

You've got a right to free speech, and you exercise that right more than anyone else you know. Whether it's about politics, humanitarian stuff, feminist issues, or just random events around you, you like to speak your mind. Hey, you've got a philosophy to espouse, a soapbox speech to make, an agenda to announce!

But how do you speak your mind when your frequent letters to the editor go unprinted, your coworkers roll their eyes at you, and your friends have started screening your calls? Print up your own newsletter or 'zine from your computer and distribute it to your like-minded citizens! Got a beef with the local meat-packing plant and want to spread the word about possible environmental concerns? Write something up to raise awareness in your community. Crazy about organic gardening and want to share tips with fellow green thumbs? Publish a regular list of tips to give people the dirt on gardening.

Being the master of your own publication, regardless of how small an audience it might target, gives you the rare opportunity to present your info in just the right context, with just the right graphics. With the desktop

> "Let us go forth not as defenders of the status quo, but as crusaders with a revolution idea . . . that the purpose of a free press is to liberate, not enslave, the human spirit."
>
> —A. S. Hills, former president of the Inter-American Press Association

publishing software that exists today, you barely have to be computer literate to crank out a decent-looking newsletter. If you want to make it even simpler, "desktop publishing" for you could mean scrawling your message by hand and photocopying it on bright paper for distribution.

If you create your own publication and it touches on a hot topic that others are interested in, you could develop a healthy following of fans who subscribe to your little publication. Before you know it, your basement newsletter might be wildly in demand faster than you can say "national circulation."

Think that sounds awfully pie in the sky? Years ago, Ariel Gore started a magazine called *Hip Mama* to address the concerns of young

mothers. *Hip Mama*'s message caught on, and it has since blossomed into a very successful regular publication and website—and it all started as a lowly little 'zine.

Not that the entire nation will be interested in getting the latest issue of your publication "Monthly Crafts to Make with Tin Cans," but you never know.

 Ladies, Start Your Engines!

✳ Check out www.zinebook.com for all sorts of 'zine-related resources.

✳ Check with your community college for classes on building your skills in desktop publishing. The better your publication looks, the more people will want to read it!

✳ There are plenty of "e-zines," or electronic magazines, on the Internet. Put your 'zine on the Web to save paper and increase its exposure.

96

Mom's Moonshine Hut

Set up a still and brew your own booze.

Have you noticed the price of quality liquor lately? Pop into your local liquor store and you can easily blow a wad of cash on two measly bottles of booze. Now you can have all the alcohol-induced fun without enduring liquor-store fleecing by brewing your booze at home!

Whether your pleasure ranges from rotgut in a jug to top-shelf scotch in a crystal snifter, homemade booze is a blast to make. And we're not talking about stuff from a still, although if you're fixin' to set up a moonshine operation with Cletus and Buford in the abandoned outhouse, knock yourself out. If your taste is decidedly less hillbilly, you're in luck. You can easily create dead ringer versions of the liqueurs you know and love, like Bailey's Irish Cream, Peppermint Schnapps, and Kahlúa, at a fraction of the price of the real stuff.

Want more reasons? D.I.Y. booze makes a great gift and a bargain buzz! It gives you a chance to be creative in the kitchen without the typical pesky domestic drawbacks, including garlicky hands, complicated recipes, or food-encrusted frying pans. It's great to have homemade liqueur on hand to serve a hot date after dinner. As Potential New Love ooooohs and aaaaahs over dinner and subsequent cordials, you can blithely say, "I made the liqueur myself. I'm a bit of an alcohol alchemist. Me, a Renaissance woman?! Oh, stop!"

You can even make up your own drinks and give them cool names!

> "Tobacco and alcohol, delicious fathers of abiding friendships and fertile reveries."
>
> —Luis Buñuel

Cleverly named concoctions such as Sex on the Beach, Flaming Dr. Pepper, and Slippery Nipple made with liquors called Vampire's Blood or Cactus Juice will pale in comparison to your Wanda's Wicked Whistle-Wetter or the Balls-Out Buzzfest. Just think—if your drink catches on, barflies the world over may someday say, "Man, I think I had one too many Screaming Naked Nectars last night."

Most liqueurs don't require too much equipment to start. For most recipes you can use just a few basic ingredients, the base alcohol, and fruit essences. If you're a hard-core chick and think it would be cool to set up a still for moonshine or corn whiskey, you should probably reconsider. At the least it's highly flammable and at most it might be illegal. Anyway, you don't want to be stuck with twenty gallons of stuff that tastes like race-car fuel if it doesn't work! Although it *could* serve as a lifetime supply of toilet disinfectant.

 Ladies, Start Your Engines!

✻ Read the book *How to Make Quality Liqueurs and Cordials at Home* by Brent Hueser.

✻ Pick up a copy of the book *The Best 50 Homemade Liqueurs* by Dona Meilach.

✻ Try out this terrific recipe for Dandelion Wine from http://recipes.alastra.com.

Dandelion Wine

1 gallon dandelion blossoms	3 oranges, peeled and sliced
1 gallon hot water	4 pounds sugar
juice of 1 lemon	1 cake of yeast

Combine water and blossoms in a crock pot. Let stand for twenty-four hours, then strain. Add the rest of the ingredients. Let the mixture sit for three weeks, then bottle. Age in bottles for at least two months before drinking.

Yield: About 1 gallon

✻ For the scoop on how to brew beer, turn to Chapter 85.

97

Do You Have Any Shoes with a Slight Wedge Heel?

Join a ladies' bowling team or go solo on a nonleague day.

Think bowling is just for men and chain-smoking, curler-wearing housewives? Think again! Bowling is back and bigger than ever—and, unlike golf or polo, it's a relatively inexpensive form of entertainment.

If you're assuming you're too old, weak, or uncoordinated to play a game that requires gliding a heavy ball down a long lane, you'll be happy to know that today's bowling balls are made with lighter material than they were fifty years ago. No more lugging a meteor-size rock from home to alley and no more sparks flying from your muffler as the back end of your car drags on the ground. Today's bowling balls have been adapted to allow even the most petite women to carry, lift, and aim with ease.

Stop by your neighborhood alley and sign up for a game. It's usually a couple bucks for one round and a dollar or two for shoe rentals, no matter how many games you play. Check out the ladies' rack. No, not the cashier's boobs, the rack of ladies' bowling balls! Pick up a few until you find the right fit for your strength and finger size. (Warning: Too small of a ball may leave your fingers stuck in the holes and you hurtling headfirst toward the pins.) Once you find your size, take a few practice runs. You're normally allowed a few warm-ups before your game. Take a few steps and swing the ball gently without releasing it, just to

> "The person who knows how to laugh at himself will never cease to be amused."
>
> —Shirley MacLaine

give yourself a feel for the rhythm of your approach. If there are other players around, watch them carefully and note their approach. Beware of the wolf in sheep's clothing, though. You don't want to mimic a frequent gutter baller just because he owns his own bowling shoes!

Once you get the "swing" of things, start your game. Head in without expectations and you're more likely to knock down some pins. You may want to brush up on score keeping *before* you get to the alley to avoid taking up a lane for three hours while you study the directions on the overhead. If you flunked basic math, you'll probably hate bowling for the sheer addition involved. Luckily, if you join a league, someone else can do the scoring.

Until then, just have fun playing and don't worry about the numbers. Unless you've played before or have an incredible streak of beginner's luck, you probably won't have a score worth bragging about anyway.

 Ladies, Start Your Engines!

❊ Want to get started on learning the basics? Check out *The Strike Zone: Bowling for Everyone* by Carol J. Blassingame or *Bowling Basics: A Step by Step Approach* by Gerald P. Carlson and E. Harold Blackwell.

❊ Are you a New Age guru trapped in ugly shoes? Jack Heise explains the hip way to improve your game in his book *How You Can Bowl Better Using Self-Hypnosis*.

❊ Think you already know enough to talk smack with the big boys? Compare your knowledge with Dawson Taylor's book *How to Talk Bowling*.

98

I Now Pronounce You the Uninvited Guest

Crash a wedding reception for the free booze and buffet.

It's a Saturday afternoon in June, the height of wedding season. At 205
Ramadas and Holiday Inns all over town, thousands of banquet workers are scurrying around, making last-minute preparations for the
numerous wedding receptions scheduled for the day. The tacky crepe
paper wedding-bell centerpieces are carefully arranged on each table,
the majestic DJ booth stands ready to spin '70s disco tunes, and the
portly roast beef guy takes his place at the buffet line, his smiling face
aglow with the orange heat lamp.

Hey, come to think of it, you like roast beef! You like '70s disco
tunes! And you most certainly like ogling groomsmen in tuxes! Forget the fact that you weren't invited. Slip into a dress and heels and go
crash a wedding reception—before you lose your nerve or talk yourself out of it! It's as easy as crashing a party in college, but without a
keg in the tub and drunken frat boys passed out on the lawn.

Is crashing a wedding reception tacky? Sure. Is it obnoxious to gobble up free food and booze at an event that people intended for their
loved ones? Without a doubt. But it's totally harmless mischief! If these
big, splashy receptions were really intended for intimate friends and
family, why would couples invite four
hundred people? C'mon, how many
"close personal friends" could they possibly have? Plus, the very fact that you
want to be there makes you a better guest

> **"A nudist wedding makes the
> best man easy to identify."**
>
> —Unknown

than Cousin Meredith's date, who in his words "got drug to this damn thing, even though she knows I hate weddings" and spends the whole afternoon passing the time by mentally undressing the bridesmaids.

Here's how you do it: Choose a big hotel, since they invariably host the largest receptions and you'll blend in easier. Don't even attempt to sneak into a small reception—you're sure to be noticed. Try to show up midevent after everyone's finished dinner and has moved on to drinks and dancing. This way you can mingle with the masses without having to explain your presence to a nosy tablemate during a forty-five-minute sit-down dinner. When asked who you are and how you know the bride, identify yourself as some distant hanger-on, such as a coworker of the groom's mother or the florist's cousin. It's a wedding reception—nobody's gonna suspect a thing or press you for details.

Once you're home free, kick back and enjoy. Nosh on mediocre wedding cake, toast the bride and groom from a disposable plastic champagne flute, and dance till your feet ache . . . then slip out quickly!

And if you ever get married and are planning your reception, don't forget to budget for the one reception expense that nobody thinks of— bouncers!

 Ladies, Start Your Engines!

※ Don't get drunk and make a scene—you're bound to get busted!

※ Don't tell your friends you crashed a wedding. Just because you *did* something tacky doesn't mean everyone has to *know* you did something tacky.

※ If you see a roaming videographer capturing everyone's well wishes on film, run the other way! You don't want to get caught on tape saying, "Congratulations, what's-his-face and what's-her-name!"

99

My Name Is Jane, and I'm a Readaholic

Join a book club or a writer's group at your local library or bookstore.

If you consider your dream day to be one spent nestled in bed with a stack of books or a pen and paper, it may be time to break out of your shell and meet others who share your addiction to escaping from reality.

A writer's group or a book club is sure to shed some light on the fact that you are not alone. Like you, some of the most normal-looking, good citizens of our communities are actually closet book junkies or frequent scribblers, cursed to a life of hidden joys due to society's misunderstandings. Labeled "bookworms," "freaks and geeks," and even "lit jockeys," today's escapists find comfort in a world of altered reality by submerging themselves in short stories, poetry, and novels— through reading, writing, or a combination of both.

Why not admit your need for acceptance and seek out a group of like-minded souls? Your local library or bookstore is sure to list a calendar of meetings and lectures specially geared to fit different interests. From critiquing the modern-day mystery to writing your biography, the possibilities are endless, thereby leaving you with no excuse for not reaching out for help.

If, in all honesty, you cannot find your one true passion (translating ancient Sanskrit into contemporary haiku may be tough), then by all means, start your own gathering!

> "She is too fond of books, and it has turned her brain."
>
> —Louisa May Alcott

207

You'll no doubt help another read- or write-aholic find the peace of mind that comes only with admission and support. "Hi, my name is Karen, and I'm a write-aholic. I toss out poetry on cocktail napkins, short stories on paper towels. Once I even wrote an essay on the back of my income tax form!"

Despite the endless list of nicknames, there's no shame in such educational addictions. Reading is fundamental, writing is cathartic, and reading your own writing, especially out loud to a group, can be quite empowering.

Whatever your passion, remind yourself that the first step is admitting you have a problem. The rest of the six-step program, however, requires going a bit deeper in your search for well-being. Here are a few of the steps to prepare you for your first support group:

Step 2: Make amends to all those friends you canceled on in lieu of leaving behind a good book every Saturday night last year.

Step 3: Take out a second mortgage to cover library fines.

Step 4: Learn to forgive filmmakers who butcher bestselling books.

Step 5: Give up hope that Kevin Costner will be able to pull off the twenty-six-year-old lead character in your novel.

Step 6: Stop hiding books all over your house.

And the most important step? Do not incorporate members of your support group into characters in your next story, especially if you plan to read it at the next meeting!

 Ladies, Start Your Engines!

✳ Call your local library or some larger bookstores to ask if they have a room you can use for your book group meetings.

✳ Ask about listing your group in the facility's newsletter. Free advertising!

✳ Be sure to designate a back-up leader if you can't make the group one night.

✳ If your bookstore of choice has a café, ask about free coffee. Many will offer coffee to support the group in hope that book sales to your members will cancel out the cost of a pot.

100

I'm Here, You're Queer

Kick up your heels at a local gay club.

If you're a chick who likes chicks, you've probably "been there, done that." But if you're a chick who likes guys and doesn't have gay friends, chances are you've never been to a gay bar before. That is, unless you accidentally wandered into a watering hole one day and noticed that, oddly enough, you were the only female in a room of two hundred men.

But why do straight people (a.k.a. "breeders") avoid gay bars? Is it that they don't think they will be welcome in a gay bar? Is it that people feel apprehensive about going to a place where they will be in the minority? Whatever the reason, it's too bad, because there's a big, gay world of cool bars for those willing to venture out!

Sociologists say that an average of 10 percent of the world population is homosexual—why not see how the other half (or rather, 10 percent) live? Even if you're a total Helen Homophobe, the only thing you have to lose is a few hours of your time and perhaps some preconceived notions. Don't rely on stereotypes gleaned from the movies and expect everyone in a gay men's bar to be decked out in leather.

Gay bars, like straight bars, can be just about anything, from quiet, friendly little neighborhood joints to country dance bars to superslick dance clubs. You won't know until you go.

If you're worried about looking conspicuous as the only woman in a room

> "If homosexuality is a disease, let's all call in queer to work. 'Hello, can't work today. Still queer.'"
> —Robin Taylor

full of guys, relax. More than likely you won't be the only female, and besides, nobody will be paying attention to you! That's the cool thing about gay bars—you can party and relax without feeling like you're on display, like you do at hetero, "meat-market" clubs. A lesbian bar might be a different story. Still, don't think everyone's staring at your ass when you make your way to the restroom—they might just be admiring your chic dark blue jeans!

But how do you find a gay bar if you aren't gay? Ask a gay friend if he or she would be willing to take you along on a night of clubbing just for the hell of it. Or call the Gay and Lesbian Chamber of Commerce in your city for more details on the various clubs and dance halls that cater to gay clientele in your town.

Another great source of details on venues are alternative newspapers, which are ususally free and can be found in many locations around town. Pick one up and flip through the "bar" section. Some papers have a specific section for gay bars, which may list more details, such as whether the club caters to lesbians, gay men, or a mixed crowd.

Patronize gay bars long enough and you just might discover a favorite new hangout! And someday, if you're straight, someone might even flatter you with the compliment "you're pretty cool, for a breeder chick."

 Ladies, Start Your Engines!

✳ Read the book *Homophobia: How We All Pay the Price* by Warren Blumenfeld. It's a varied collection of essays about gays and straights written by both men and women.

✳ If you're choosing songs from a jukebox in a lesbian bar, don't ask in a big loud voice, "Hey, how come all this jukebox plays is Melissa Etheridge and the Indigo Girls?"

✳ As for all you lesbians who haven't been to a straight bar in a while, get out there. It could be a nice change of pace.

101

Ladies' Card Night

Start a chicks-only poker or bridge club.

Welcome to chicks' poker night. Time to mix yourself a stiff Vodka gimlet, light a fat cigar, and assume your most convincing poker face! (Chomping on bologna sandwiches and sitting around a wobbly kitchen table in your undershirt is optional.)

Card games such as bridge and poker seem to be a bit yesteryear when it comes to entertainment these days. Sadly, cool card games like five-card draw and Shanghai have been largely eclipsed in younger generations by cable reruns and boob tube schlock. Why not revive cards as the great American pastime by starting your own bridge or poker club? A weekly card game is not only a fun excuse for hanging with your chums on a regular basis, it's a good mental workout as well—and a surefire way to pick up a little cash under the table, if you're a betting broad.

If you're convinced bridge is something timid little grannies play while sitting around in hot pink gabardine culottes and waiting for their rollers to dry, think again. Sure, bridge has a reputation akin to shuffleboard and bingo as an old-folk's game. Let's face it, how many hip young things do you hear saying, "Screw spinning class, I'm up for a game of bridge!" But give cards a chance to get into your blood, and soon you'll be shuffling a mean

> "Last night I stayed up late playing poker with tarot cards. I got a full house and four people died."
>
> —Stephen Wright

casino-style deck and spouting game lingo like "K-Q trumps" and "ruffing a diamond" just as generations of Bridge Club Betties have before you.

If you don't know the first thing about bridge, pick up one of the many books or video beginner's guides to bridge (or poker, if that's more your style). Since the game rules rarely change, you can also find a copy of an old bridge guide at any used book store or thrift shop for practically nothing. Better yet, ask your grandma if you can sit in as an alternate at her bridge game for tips on the finer points of the game.

Once you learn the ropes, how do you start a club? Put up notices at local gaming shops or recruit some of your card-playing pals. You need only four bridge players to get things started; spread the word among friends and coworkers, and you're sure to be the queen of your very own card clique in no time. Pick a weekly or bimonthly meeting time and designate it as card night. Then dust off that card table in the basement and get those shuffling fingers limbered up!

And as they say in Vegas, have a lucky day.

 Ladies, Start Your Engines!

✽ Visit the American Contract Bridge League at www.acbl.org for more links and resources than you can shake an ace of spades at!

✽ No one's interested in playing bridge in your area? Join an on-line game! Visit www.thehouseofcards.com for rules and links.

✽ Been wondering when you'd have the chance to wear those tacky dice earrings your aunt bought you in Vegas? Now is the time!

102

Frequent Flyer Miles Davis

Take advantage of a cheap weekend flight to a city known for great music.

It's Friday night, Anywhere, USA. You know the drill: You call your girlfriends and agree on a bar to kick off the weekend. "Somewhere fun and different" are usually the only requirements. Three hours later, you're tarted up in vampy lipliner and a lace Miracle Bra, getting your toes pulverized by some rhythmically challenged dork on the dance floor as you endure the same lame set of crappy cover songs from an off-tune garage band that should have stayed in the garage. You broke out your Miracle Bra for this?!

Time to blow off the tired local scene and jet to a spot where the music is *really* happening, which means you'll have to get on a plane and go somewhere else, unless you're lucky enough to live in Austin, New Orleans, or San Francisco. Fly to a destination where the joints are jumping, the bands are rockin', and the rhythmically challenged are forced off the dance floor.

Sounds like too much of a splurge for a fun-filled weekend? Don't back out now, party girl! Plan ahead to nab a great weekend deal and talk a friend or two into going with you to split hotel costs. Zillions of cheap airline seats can be found last minute, too, just by calling your local travel agent or checking Internet travel sites. It takes only a Friday afternoon off to hit your town of choice by Friday night.

Keep your eyes peeled for a killer deal to a happenin' town advertised in your

> "Music washes away from the soul the dust of everyday life."
>
> —Red Auerbach

local paper, and plan to go in January or February, when everyone's broke from the holidays and airline tix are cheapest. The only things left to do are book a few nights at a hotel close to the action, check the local club listings on-line for weekend entertainment, and get ready to have a blast! Don't forget these essentials for your tune-filled weekend:

* Gobs of cash in small bills—Drinks at the Bahia Cabana in San Francisco ain't cheap, and cover charges add up when you're club hopping.

* The perfect shoes—As luck would have it, you might find yourself looking at your portable city guide of downtown only to find out that the *really* hot club is ten blocks away. If you are one of the lucky women who has a single pair of shoes that are comfy enough to walk in yet funky enough to go out in, pack 'em. Do your bunions a favor and skip the four-inch stilettos for this trip!

* Disposable camera—Sure, you'll feel like a goofy Midwestern huckster snapping pictures in a tony club, but sixty seconds of awkwardness is worth capturing the party weekend of a lifetime. Take disposable only, so you won't be heartbroken if it breaks, gets beer splashed on it, or gets stolen. It will be the proof to your pals back home that you chatted up Brian Setzer over Budweisers during his band break!

 Ladies, Start Your Engines!

* Check out airline websites for great deals on last-minute weekend flights.

* Save the ticket stubs and flyers you collect as mementos of your whirlwind party weekend.

* Pack light! Getting a stiff neck from lugging too much stuff through the airport will spoil the fun.

* Pack your earplugs, if not for the music played at deafening levels at some clubs, then to block out the traffic noise when you're trying to sleep at the hotel.

103

Annie Get Your Gun

Have some Old West pictures taken at a carnival.

It's summertime and the carnival is here! That doesn't just mean flies   215
stuck to the cotton candy dispenser, rigged ring-toss games, and the
smell of vomit wafting from the direction of the Tilt-O-Whirl. The carnival means old-time photos!

You've probably seen these old-time photos. They're the antique-
looking sepia-toned portraits cranked out from a carnival booth, complete with period costumes and phony props. These pictures *look* like
old-time frontier photographs (you can almost smell the horse manure
and dust from the plains!), but they're about as genuine Old West as
the Hollywood prop facades from those Clint Eastwood western flicks.
The staff dresses you up in fishnets, turn-of-the-century hats, and
garter belts like Miss Kitty, then snaps your smile as you lean up
against a saloon door or antique bar. They slap the photo into an equally
phony antique matte frame and off you go.

Need a few ideas to liven it up? Go with a gaggle of girls and pose
in corsets and feather boas to look like the whorehouse welcoming
committee! Dress yourself as a gunslinger and pose solo. Maybe they
can even add a little coffee-grounds "stubble" to your face to complete
the look! Or go with a date and pose as a gunslinging couple. It never
fails that five years after you break up, you'll find this picture at the bottom of a desk drawer and think to
yourself nostalgically, "Cheap, flaky,
and a bad kisser, but what a dashing
gunslinger!"

> "Say cheese!"
> —Anonymous

Hang up your old-time photo at home and try to convince naive houseguests it's an actual photo of your ancestors. "My great aunt was Little Annie Oakley, and this picture of her in a frontier watering hole with Buffalo Bill proves it. Can't you see the resemblance?"

Can't wait for the carnival to arrive or you live in a town the carnival doesn't come to? No problem! Plenty of companies can add a sepia tint to your existing photographs for an antique look. (However, unless you happen to have an 1800s hoop skirt and parasol lying around your house, period costuming might be a problem.) You can even purchase sepia-tint film and load it into your own camera if you're so inclined.

Better yet, pop into a photo booth at your local mall or amusement park. Just feed in four quarters, close the curtain, and smile for the camera. Where else can you get four pictures taken for a buck?

 Ladies, Start Your Engines!

✳ Hang your photo in a beat-up old frame for added visual impact.

✳ If you're on the East Coast and you'd rather visit a studio for your old-time photo, visit www.oldtimephotos.com for studio locations. If you live somewhere else, the phone book is a good place to start.

✳ Get ready for a whole new appreciation of modern clothing. Fifteen minutes cinched into a costume corset will make you glad you weren't born an 1800s-era saloon girl.

104

Diamonds Are a Girl's Best Friend

Make your own jewelry.

If you've ever purchased a "gold" bracelet from the flea market after the salesman swore it was a solid, fourteen-karat steal only to have it turn your wrist green as soon as you got it home, you know that "all that glitters is not gold" isn't just a cliché. Still, practically every chick (besides the absolute minimalists among us) really goes for a little adornment now and then. From noisy charm bracelets to funky bangles, delicate glass beadery to a multicarat monster solitaire, a world of beautiful baubles awaits you!

Jewelry is an accessory that can be a true expression of the wearer's personality and style. One girl's precious charm may be another girl's eyesore. Case in point: Ask a tree-hugging Deadhead hippy chick to trade trinkets with a bleach-blond Texas beauty queen and mayhem will ensue, with hippy chick disdaining her diamond and ruby cocktail sparkler as an oppressive symbol of mainstream materialism and big Tex bitching about how woven hemp bracelets give her a rash.

Ever go out for a night on the town, feeling like hot stuff until you run into some chick at a party wearing the exact same earrings and necklace? You're not the only one who happened to catch the "75 percent off Sterling Silver Sale" at Nordstrom last weekend! Avoid such awkward situations by making your own jewelry!

Jewelry making isn't as difficult as it sounds. Plenty of craft stores and bead

> "One should either be a work of art or wear a work of art."
>
> —Oscar Wilde

supply shops sell all the jewelry-making materials you need, from wires and clasps to glass and clay beads in a zillion colors and designs. And plenty of weaving shops out there sell stuff to make earthy-looking jewelry like friendship bracelets and woven chokers. If working with precious gems sounds more like your thing, drop by a jewelry-making class and find out how to select and set stones.

Make your own unique jewelry and soon you'll be the envy of your friends and coworkers. Next time they start ooohing and aaahing over your one-of-a-kind necklace, you can silently congratulate yourself for being a stellar jewelry designer.

 Ladies, Start Your Engines!

✳ Pick up the book *Beads: Make Your Own Unique Jewelry* by Stefany Tomalin or *Creative Clay Jewelry: Extraordinary Colorful Fun Designs to Make from Polymer Clay* by Leslie Dierks.

✳ Troll junk stores and trinket shops for old jewelry so you can recycle the parts, such as beads and clasps.

✳ Gather your basic jewelry-making tools before you start. Tweezers, small wire cutters, a needle for stringing beads, and a divided tray or pillbox to keep beads separate are all helpful.

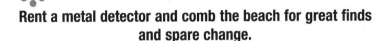

105

She Sells Seashells by the Seashore

Rent a metal detector and comb the beach for great finds and spare change.

Ready to find stuff on the beach you never even knew existed? A world of interesting discoveries awaits you just under the sand, revealed with the help of a metal detector.

If you've ever combed Venice Beach or similar oceanfront stretches, probably the only "discoveries" you've made have been used condom wrappers, dirty Big Gulp cups, and more dead fish than you could count. But with a metal detector, a wealth of old rusty padlocks, coins, watches, and World War II dog tags are waiting for you to discover! With a superhigh-quality metal detector, you could really score and find a jewel-encrusted treasure chest, brought over by Spanish explorers, overflowing with gold coins and jewels—or perhaps the masthead from the Mayflower! OK, that's probably an exaggeration. You'll find more pop-can tabs than plundered pirate golden earrings, but it will still be fun!

Hey, searching for treasure beats baking in the sun like a raisin, even if you don't find anything. You'll be wandering around getting some exercise while all the other beach dwellers bake in a pool of tanning oil getting skin cancer. And it would provide a great opening line if you happen upon some bodybuilder hottie working out on the beach. Here are a few choice pick-up lines to get you started:

> "I have the world's largest collection of seashells. I keep it on all the beaches of the world . . . perhaps you've seen it."
> —Stephen Wright

* "This metal detector must really work . . . it seems to have found me an iron man."
* "This isn't a metal detector, it's a beefcake tracker!"
* "Here, tuck this metal coin down your shorts and we'll see if my metal detector can pinpoint its exact location."
* "Oh no, the magnet on my metal detector seems to have sucked up your car keys! I'd be happy to give them back in exchange for your number."

If you can afford it, buy a metal detector instead of renting one. The crappy metal detectors found in rental shops have been used and abused to their limits and can barely find a tin can two inches away. You need a metal detector that can actually detect metal. Plus, every well-equipped bachelorette pad needs a metal detector. You wouldn't think so, but it just might come in handy. Not only for more beach junking, either. Lost an earring in the shag carpet? Gold bracelet broke off somewhere in the backyard and you can't find it? Feel like digging up the "space capsule" coffee can you and your brother buried under your parents' apple tree twenty years ago? It's Metal Detector to the rescue!

 Ladies, Start Your Engines!

* Get a screaming deal on a used detector by visiting an on-line auction site such as www.ubid.com or www.ebay.com.

* Believe it or not, metal-detector makers also manufacture scads of accessories. Visit www.discountdetector.com for bags and recovery tools.

* If you dig up that space capsule, be sure to give your brother's "I Love Debbie Simmons" note and pet rock back to him for a good laugh.

106

You Deserve a Day Off

Call in sick!

Unless you are independently wealthy or some rich dead relative leaves you a bunch of money, it's likely that you'll be holding down a job for many years to come. And unless you are a professional stunt woman, chocolate taste tester, or rock star, your job probably isn't all that fun or exciting (that's why they have to pay you to show up!).

Even if you don't hate your job, you still deserve a day of freedom! Why not cash in and play one of the few aces that workers have, the personal day? If you're feeling a little sick—of working—use that hard-earned sick day. Call your boss, feign a twenty-four-hour flu, then order a pizza and watch daytime TV in your bathrobe and bunny slippers!

If you feel guilty fibbing to your boss, get over it. The world won't collapse if you miss a day. And besides, just because you're not lying on your death bed doesn't mean you couldn't use a little mental-health break! If you don't feel like using the typical standby excuses (got a cold, car won't start), feel free to use one of these uniquely indisputable excuses:

* "I'm a member of an obscure and mysterious all-female voodoo cult. We celebrate the lunar solstice by retreating into the woods on the first Monday of the month to revere the goddess Uterine with a pagan sacrifice ceremony."

> "If you get to thirty-five and your job still involves wearing a name tag, you've probably made a serious vocational error."
>
> —Dennis Miller

* "The next-door neighbor I carpool with went crazy and is holed up in his house with a bomb strapped to his chest. The SWAT team has our whole block surrounded!"

* "In celebration of National Donut Day, I ate a dozen bearclaws and am now in a state of frosting-fueled hysteria, too hopped up on sugar to drive."

So, you've called in, now what? First off, don't even think about showering! You've got nowhere to go, so there's no need to smell good or wear makeup. Indulge in an all-out spoil-yourself day, starting with a big, gooey breakfast (perhaps you really do want to eat a dozen bearclaws!). Get caught up on that hot new fiction novel you checked out from the library and have been dying to start reading.

Or, convince a friend to call in sick too. Then you can meet for lunch and hang out all day playing hooky. You're *such* a bad influence! Being naughty is always more fun if there's someone to share it with. Maybe the two of you could work on your "day after calling in sick" act. You know the one: the next day, everyone asks how you're feeling and you smile sheepishly, fake a cough, and croak, "Um, OK, I guess . . ."

 Ladies, Start Your Engines!

* Allow yourself to feel guilty about calling in for no more than ten seconds—your office will not crumble if you take a day off!

* Take the phone off the hook so your boss doesn't call every hour asking where some file is.

* Look pallid and dress crappy the day you return to work so people will think you really were sick.

107

Corningware, Shmorningware

✳

Paint your own plates.

Dishes are a basic necessity of domestic life. Besides furniture, dishes are probably one of the first things you purchased when you got your own place. Or maybe you still use that Corningware stuff with the little daisies on it that Mom gave you when you moved out, along with a chocolate-brown sectional couch from the basement and a mirrored coffee table!

You know you've finally made that transition into adulthood when you find yourself in the kitchenware department of a store saying, "A floral pattern is too busy—I like the southwestern look" and "I need something practical enough for everyday, but with a bit of flair for entertaining." Hey, you're a grown woman now, and it's time to toss those coffee-stained mugs, garage sale plates, and gas-station plastic beverage tumblers you call drinking glasses, and buy some *real* dishes!

If you're tired of eating off the same crummy chipped plates you bought as a four-piece set from Kmart for $12.99, it's time for an upgrade. Even if the most sophisticated fare you serve is Chef Boyardee straight from the can, new dishes are a great way to dress up the presentation. SpaghettiOs can practically pass for "pasta rings in rich tomato sauce" when served in an elegant china bowl!

For truly dazzling dishes, forget buying. Instead, visit a paint-it-

> "I hate housework. You do the dishes and six months later you have to start all over again."
> —Joan Rivers

yourself ceramic studio and create a dish set that is uniquely you. Paint-it-yourself ceramic studios sell unpainted, unglazed pieces that serve as a blank canvas. The studio also provides plenty of paints and space for you to go crazy. Once you give those pieces the Picasso treatment, the studio fires and glazes them for you. Voila, custom dishes! You'll have a set of serving ware that's true to your taste, without resorting to buying a boring set from the department store. You'll have dishes that reflect your personality (just try finding purple dishes with black polka dots in a store!), and you will be able to set a mighty fine look-ing table the next time company comes over.

Your new dishware is sure to make you feel like a true domestic goddess and keep you happily stocked with saucers and such for years to come. Now if someone would just invent dishes that wash themselves . . .

 Ladies, Start Your Engines!

✻ If you live in Los Angeles, visit the Ceramic Art Space for scads of greenware and a "frequent firer's club." Call them at 818-752-9767.

✻ Visit Seattle's Painted Fire for unglazed pieces, mosaic tile classes, and monthly workshops, plus a potter's wheel if you want to throw clay yourself. For more information, call 206-545-2816.

✻ Go to the tiny Ceramic Pineapple studio in Denver, which offers pieces to paint and hosts birthday painting parties for kids and adults. Call 303-458-7491 for details.

108

A Picture's Worth a Thousand Words

Make your own postcards or stationery and impress your long-distance friends.

E-mail, cell phones, and beepers seem to have taken control of our communications, holding us electronically hostage from one another as we make contact without really being in touch. For a more personal touch, why not write letters instead? The letters you send today can become tomorrow's treasured mementos—just try saying that about an E-mail message.

The paper you use can be an expression of a feeling or thought in itself before you write a single word. There's no shortage of store-bought stationery available, but finding "just the right stuff" for your purpose can be exasperating. You search for sophisticated thank-you notes only to find everything's junked up with teddy bears, and you can't find bridal shower invites that don't print a gushy, gag-inducing poetry verse inside.

For a unique look, how about making your own stationery or embellishing the plain paper you already have? You can create your own invitations, letterhead, and envelopes in designs limited only by your imagination (and perhaps by U.S. Post Office mailing regulations).

The possibilities are endless. Throwing a cocktail party? Handwrite the party details on a cocktail napkin and send it out. Need to keep in touch with your family back home? Use snapshots of yourself as postcards. Just mount a smiling

> "To send a letter is a good way to go somewhere without moving anything but your heart."
>
> —Phyllis Theroux

225

picture of yourself on the back of a blank postcard and ship it off—now maybe your Grandma will stop grumbling that you never send her any pictures. Or throw a Chinese food dinner for friends and turn a paper fan into the invitation.

Once you've created a paper masterpiece, there's no sense sending it off in a ho-hum envelope. Use paper lunch bags instead—all you need to do is cut the top to create a flap and close it up with a sticker or wax seal. Another possibility: Take two different kinds of paper and stitch them together on a regular sewing machine to form an envelope. It won't be long before you earn a reputation as the Martha Stewart of stationery.

 Ladies, Start Your Engines!

✳ Check with the U.S. Post Office to be sure your homemade envelopes are suitable for mailing—you don't want your stuff to arrive ripped up and shredded!

✳ Pick up the book *The Art of Creative Lettering: 50 Amazing Fonts You Can Make for Scrapbooks, Cards, Invitations, and Signs* by Becky Higgins and Siobhan McGowan.

✳ Keep your eye on the various craft shows on TV for the latest trends in stationery design.

109

Your Mama's So Fat . . .

Gather your best material for a night as a stand-up comedian.

Ever been to a comedy club laughing along with the crowd at the brave yuckster on stage and wished it could be you? Well, funny girl, thanks to amateur night at your local comedy club, that really could be you!

As a budding Chris Rock, Rita Rudner, or Bill Maher, there's a spot for you on stage. Roseanne started doing stand-up comedy as a housewife many years ago and look at her now! Of course, your comedy style may not bag you a hit prime-time comedy series, talk show host gig, and six-figure wardrobe budget, but it might generate some sincere applause and a free comedy club T-shirt.

Don't be intimidated by being on stage! Chances are there won't be a huge audience in attendance on amateur night, and since it's showcasing new talent (or lack thereof), everyone's sure to be gentle with you. Think of it this way: You are there to give the hardworking folks in attendance the gift of a giggle or two, so don't be too hard on yourself if you don't get a standing ovation. Don't sweat it and have a great time. If you've ever told a kooky story and had your coworkers rolling in the aisle, you know what it's like to put on a performance. Now take your act away from the water cooler and put it under a spotlight!

Call local clubs and find out what the guidelines are for amateur night. You might be asked to submit a tape of your material before being allowed on stage. To get yourself into the performance mind-set, deliver your material onto a tape recorder so

> "Nobody ever died of laughter."
> —**Max Beerbohm**

you can play it back and tighten up your routine (you know—to work out the stammers and slow spots). Taping yourself first is also a great way to time your routine, in case the stage manager wants to know how long you plan on keeping 'em gripping their bellies in a fit of hilarity.

Before getting on stage, attend amateur night to see what kinds of acts perform at that club. You might be a nervous wreck before you go only to discover you are far more entertaining than the middle-aged computer salesman who does a ten-minute bit on what a bummer it is being bald and flatulent or the bungling prop comic who keeps dropping stuff when he's trying to juggle. Chat with other budding comics for tips and work on your material in front of a mirror to sharpen your delivery.

And if worse comes to worse, cross your fingers that there's someone really goofy looking in the front row whom you can make fun of to take the pressure off!

 Ladies, Start Your Engines!

✳ Pick up a copy of *How to Be a Working Comic: An Insider's Guide to a Career in Stand-Up Comedy* by Dave Schwensen.

✳ Study at home with *Sandi Cee Shore's "Sandbox" Stand-Up Comedy Home Study Course System*, available through Amazon.com.

✳ Study the queens of comedy—rent copies of "The Carol Burnett Show," "I Love Lucy" episodes, or Joan Rivers's routines on tape.

110

Step In as Meg Ryan's Foot Double

Be an extra for a film shooting near your town.

If you've longed to hear a director shout, "Lights, camera, action!" but have the acting skills of a doormat, don't give up hope of being in the movies. Hundreds of films need background folks to fill in the space behind the stars, whether it's a street scene, a restaurant shot, or a bleacher full of baseball fans.

Fill in as an extra, and you'll be the envy of all your friends when you announce that you were in the latest Brad Pitt flick. "Yeah, that's me, the blonde walking down the crowded street behind Brad. I'm on the screen for two whole seconds!" There's no talent, auditioning, or other criteria involved besides showing up, and you might even get to hang out with the stars! Or at least in reasonable proximity to them.

As an extra, don't expect to get much for your efforts. There won't be any catered lunches, professional makeup artists, or legions of fans screaming your name and sneaking into your trailer to beg for your autograph. In fact, the most you can expect for your hours of film work is twenty bucks or some token prize (movie producers assume that basking in the magical glow of celebrities is payment enough). But hey, you'll still get to be in a movie, and that's pretty exciting! Plus, you'll get an inside look at how movies are made. You may discover that Hollywood stars are regular people too, especially when filming grinds to a halt because Jodie Foster has to pee.

> "Don't judge a book by its movie."
>
> —Anonymous

Here are a few tips on how to find opportunities for extras: Keep your eyes on the bulletin board at your local film school, which may list films soon to be shot in your area. They mainly list smaller, independent films, but that might be better—chances are you'll get more screen time with a smaller picture! If you hear of a film being shot near your home, you can call the studio directly for details on how to be an extra.

And don't forget to give yourself the star treatment by ordering a folding, canvas director's chair with your name emblazoned on the back. When the movie's done filming, you can perch in your chair wearing your celeb shades and order your roommate around like a stage hand: "Stephan, my skim double latte is lukewarm. Be a dear and heat it up for me, would you?"

 Ladies, Start Your Engines!

✳ Register to be a movie extra at www.ep-services.com/html/cenex.htm.

✳ Check out www.extracast.com to enter their extra database. There's a membership fee, but so what—you're bound to be a star, baby!

✳ Practice air kissing like a true Hollywood type.

111

Kiln Time with Clay

Take out your aggressions on a mound of clay.

Pottery—one of the few artistic mediums that's still popular even though it's older than dirt (no joke—broken pottery from as far back in time as 5000 B.C. has been found in Egyptian tombs!). Maybe that's because a humble mound of clay can be molded into millions of things, from water-carrying vessels to the pyramids themselves.

Working with clay may sound a little too artsy craftsy for your taste as you recall the lumpy, side-leaning ashtray you made for your mom in first grade. But now that you're older, and perhaps more coordinated, consider all the cool things you can make, such as vases, candle holders, wall plaques, mosaic tiles, and picture frames. Plus, you can paint your finished pieces any way you like. You might even start hearing "Unchained Melody" as the spirit of Patrick Swayze sneaks up behind you to help work that clay with a sensual touch just as he did with Demi in *Ghost*. And you thought clay was boring! Try getting that kind of action in a watercolor class! Sign up to take a spin on the pottery wheel—and discover why you have to place the mound *exactly* in the center of the wheel. Hint: Fellow class-goers don't take kindly to big chunks of terra cotta hurling toward them at ninety miles per hour.

To find a class, ask around at your local art supply store. Chances are there's a local pottery prodigy who

> "All arts we practice are apprenticeships. The big art is our life."
>
> —Mary Caroline Richards, potter

231

offers classes regularly. He or she can clue you in to all the basics, from clay types to firing and glazing. Numerous other classes are held at community schools and adult education centers, which often use middle school and high school art studios when the kids are away.

So you found a class and are all hyped up to create the World's Coolest Spoonrest? That's great! Before you head out, though, be sure to wear your absolute grubbiest grubbies. Clay has a tendency to be very messy. When you're working with water to smooth the surface or to rewet the object you're working on, you'll get nasty clay juice everywhere. You should also invest in an industrial-strength nail brush while you're at it. The only thing tougher than clay to get out from under your fingernails is dried clay!

Today, a lopsided clay bowl. Tomorrow, a life-size replica of Michelangelo's *David* adorning your living room!

 Ladies, Start Your Engines!

✳ No classes offered in your area? Go to a hobby store and pick up ready-to-use clay to work with. You can make scads of stuff with ordinary clay and your own two hands.

✳ Read the book *Make It in Clay: A Beginner's Guide to Ceramics* by Charlotte F. Speight.

✳ Make your mom another lopsided ashtray, just for fun.

112

She Got Game

Join a women's basketball team.

So, the only dribbling you've done at a basketball game is over Kobe Bryant's scrumptiously defined deltoids? The only slam dunking you've done is your almond biscotti in a cup of decaf? And, the only "rebounding" you've ever done is when you went out with that freaky artist guy when your boyfriend dumped you?

Even if you've never shot a single basket, the joy of hoops can be contagious. Basketball is one of the most fast-paced, action-packed sports around, reigning supreme over lesser spectator sports. Forget football. Who wants to brave a November blizzard, shivering in rickety stadium seats while waiting for the refs to argue over an instant replay? And hockey is intense for sure, but the excitement comes more from watching toothless wahoos throwing jabs than from the actual game.

If you already think watching b-ball is fun, try playing it! Don't worry if the only time you ever run is on your way to the bathroom after downing a Big Gulp. Even if you aren't a finely tuned athlete, you can still have fun. Basketball training gets you in great shape, since it's mostly aerobic activity, and it sharpens your reflexes and builds team spirit. If you were a pudgy little bookworm in high school or more interested in being president of the thespians club and missed out on sports, now's your chance to

> "Basketball is the second most exciting indoor sport, and the other one shouldn't have spectators."
>
> —Dick Vertleib

redeem yourself. Express your inner jock! Not only will you have a chance to meet and hang with other adult players who may be new to the game, there won't be any snotty cheerleader types to make fun of you from the sidelines.

OK, so you wanna "be like Mike" and don't know where to go? Start shooting hoops on your own to build confidence and to get comfy dribbling and shooting a basketball. Every neighborhood in this country has a basketball court nearby to practice on, although you may have to muscle it away from a horde of teenage boys first. If you belong to a gym, you might already have access to a court and maybe even organized games and open court times, too. Contact your local YWCA or recreation center for details on adult basketball leagues for women.

They should be able to point you in the right direction or at least tell you when open court times are so you can show up to see if other women are playing.

Finally—a chance to push those Nike Airs to the limit by doing something besides grocery shopping on a Saturday afternoon.

 Ladies, Start Your Engines!

✱ Check out www.usabasketball.com to get psyched.

✱ Invest in a good sports bra or risk a painful case of next-day sore boobies!

✱ Go to a professional women's basketball game to see how the pros do it. Refer to www.wnba.com for details and schedules.

113

Avoid the Warm Spots

Go to a public pool and catch up on a trashy novel.

Summer's here! After surviving the winter doldrums and pounding snow, the sun you've waited patiently for has finally returned. Celebrate summer's arrival by heading to the local pool to catch some rays and tackle that saucy novel you've been meaning to read.

235

There's sure to be a pool right down the street from you no matter where you live, so dig out that bikini from the bottom of your lingerie drawer and join in the collective dread of bathing suit season. After six months of bulky sweaters, continual snacking, and no exercise, *Sports Illustrated* probably won't be calling you for their swimsuit issue, but at least you're not alone!

Ignore those pangs of dread as you locate that racy little two-piece you forgot you had and head into the bathroom to tackle that jungle growth you call a bikini line. You don't want your fellow pool-goers to flee in terror at the sight of you in high-cut bikini bottoms! While you're at it, you might be tempted to do something with those icky yellow toenails of yours (socks at the pool are a little out of place, don't you think?). Give yourself an emergency pedicure if you're the primping kind, or just blow it off. You're supposed to be enjoying some fun in the sun, not prepping for a damn beauty pageant!

If you haven't been to a public pool since you were a kid, you might be in

The bikini was invented in 1946 by two Frenchmen, Jacques Heim and Louis Reard, and named after the Bikini atoll in the Marshall Islands.

for a surprise. Gone are the days when the local pool consisted of hordes of screaming kids on summer break, splashing around and secretly peeing in the shallow end (no wonder they put in nearly toxic levels of chlorine!). Some local pools today actually have water slides, decent locker rooms, and reasonably fresh water.

If you're planning on lounging poolside for the day with your Danielle Steele sizzler, it won't matter if the water's rank or not. You'll be too busy basting yourself in a mixture of tanning oil and sweat, sipping a perfectly cold diet soda from the pop machine, and trying to strategically place yourself in the exact center of your beach towel. You're sure to return home a little tanner, a bit oilier, and much more relaxed than when you first arrived.

Now you're rested up and ready to tackle that pedicure!

 Ladies, Start Your Engines!

✳ Pack plenty of sunscreen! You don't want to kick off the summer with a nasty sunburn.

✳ Take a wide-brimmed hat to cut the glare while you're reading and add a little extra poolside "star appeal."

✳ Can't find a beach towel? Just fold up a flat white sheet or blanket to lounge on. It's easier to get tanning oil out of a sheet than it is your luxury Egyptian cotton bathroom towels.

114

Save the Snackwells

Organize a fund-raiser for your favorite charity.

Wanna ensure your seat in heaven and on the town council at the same time? Organize a fund-raiser for your favorite charity!

Raising money for a nonprofit isn't like raising Democratic campaign contributions. First of all, heartwarming foundations like the Humane Society cross party lines. (Planned Parenthood is something else entirely.) Just try to find anyone, even a seventy-year-old Republican, who can stare into the eyes of a malnourished pup without dropping a few bucks into your lap. Sure, there are always those few die-hards, the ones who are more likely to be struck by the unprovoked urge to dress in plaid and chase a tiny golf ball around acres of flat greens than give up a buck to someone who didn't earn it "the old-fashioned way." But for the most part, you can expect to hit your mark if you set some realistic goals.

First and foremost, find a charity that both interests you and needs some financial assistance. That includes just about all of them! Your local pound, homeless shelter, soup kitchen, or battered-women's shelter are always good choices. Next, set up a meeting with the director or person in charge of public relations. Explain your interests and offer a few suggestions for how you can raise some cash.

Bake sales are relatively easy to organize, but they don't tend to raise that much money. Ditto with car washes,

> "If a free society cannot help the many who are poor, it cannot save the few who are rich."
>
> —John F. Kennedy

unless you plan on flashing more than your pearly whites. Auctions often require more work to pull off, but depending on the items up for bid, you could rake in some major funds that could put you on the front page of *The Daily Samaritan*. Soliciting contributions from businesses will probably be the most difficult part of the process, and organizing volunteers, finding an auctioneer, and securing free advertising will also test your skills as a coordinator. If you can pull it off, an auction can be both lucrative and fun and you may even go home with a few bargains.

Charity balls can also be good sources of revenue; however, they're anything but easy to plan. If you're looking for immediate gratification, a ball isn't for you. They take months of planning, lots of ticket

sales, and probably cash up front to invest in the necessary details (e.g., invitations, a deposit on a large venue, booking a band, and so on).

If you're not completely discouraged by now, congratulations! You've passed the first test of commitment. Even for the most well-meaning supporter, organizing a fund-raiser can be a flash-in-the-pan idea. If you're truly dedicated to your cause, however, raising money for your favorite charity will be just the first step toward greatness. Today the town council, tomorrow the Senate!

 Ladies, Start Your Engines!

✳ Sign up for a free fund-raising newsletter at www.fundraising-ideas.com.

✳ For tasty ideas and inspirations, check out *Food Activities as a Fundraiser: A Reference* by Frieda Carol.

✳ Talk the talk while you walk the walk with *Fundraiser's Phrase Book* (for serious fund-raisers) by Gail Hamilton.

115

A Waist Is a Terrible Thing to Mind

Take a free candy-making class.

Looking for that ultimate high that won't make your urine sample the talk of the town? Enroll in a free candy-making class at a sugary shopette. Many chocolatiers are all too happy to share their "secret recipes" (for example, a melted bag of chocolate chips) in hope that you'll invest in their conveniently on-site cooking gadgets and baking ingredients.

If you're afraid that giving in to your sweet tooth means loosening your belt, remember that you can always give away your infectious confections. Candy, much like cash, makes the ultimate gift. Got a down-in-the-dumps friend who needs a quick pick-me-up? Nothing says energy like a trunk full of truffles. Or perhaps you have a penny-pinching pal who loves to tempt her fate with Death by Chocolate but is too cheap to splurge on the Fudge-of-the-Month Club. Why not drop off a semiannual array of your best penuche?

Afraid your attempts at candy making will fall short of Godiva goddessdom? You'll have no choice but to sample your homework to make sure your peanut butter clusters are up to par. Poor you!

Of course, unlike your virginity, you don't have to feel compelled to give your goodies away to the first person who shows an interest in your talents. Why not focus on practicing your savory sessions for the big leagues—you know, the day you actually have someone over for a little

> "Research tells us that 14 out of any 10 individuals like chocolate."
> —Sandra Boynton

somethin' somethin'. Not only does chocolate raise your serotonin levels to put you in the mood for some lovin', but you may actually be able to work some of your most risqué recipes into foreplay! Why not drizzle some (semicooled) chocolate onto your lover's chest? That's assuming, of course, that it's not hairy enough to cause a cocoa snarl when it dries. Or perhaps let your love lick some caramel coating off *your* sweet spots! Sure, there are flavored body gels and there's always hot wax, but who wants to be reminded that it's time to tone down your eyebrow hair again? Chocolate is so much more sensual, and it'll certainly keep a grin on your face while you listen to the candy-shop owner explain how to "harden your mold."

 Ladies, Start Your Engines!

✳ For calorie-free inspiration, pick up *Making Homemade Candy* by Glenn Andrews and Sally Sussman or *Candy-Making Basics* by Evelyn Howe Fryatt.

✳ Think you've got what it takes to run Hershey's out of business? Compare your skills to those on *Candy and Chocolate* (video).

116

Someone's in the Kitchen with Dinah

Start a family-recipe cookbook.

Mom's meatloaf, Uncle Mike's mean green chile, Grandma Lydia's sweet potato pie. Most family gatherings seem to be fueled with fabulous food, and every family has certain dishes that folks have perfected over the years for others to savor. Start a cookbook of family recipes and someday future generations may be cooking your special vegetarian lasagna!

Why make a family cookbook when there are scads and scads of cookbooks on the market? To save as a family keepsake, mainly. Collecting family recipes and creating a cookbook with them will preserve the talents and memories of the clan long after the folks who created the original recipes have passed on. It's a great way to honor family history, and it will help your children and your children's children appreciate their roots.

Plus, the entire family will be privy to all sorts of cooks' special touches. With a clan cookbook, all your great-aunts will know that the secret ingredient in Grandma's peach cobbler was a healthy shot of dark rum. Oh, and "love," of course!

Here are a few tips for creating a culinary volume that the entire kinship can use and enjoy. Solicit recipes from the *entire* family, not just the few who have reputations as cooks. Just because your cousin hasn't whipped up a batch of her outrageous oatmeal raisin cookies in decades doesn't mean she

> "My mother is such a lousy cook that Thanksgiving at her house is a time of sorrow."
> —Rita Rudner

shouldn't be included. Try to get a good mix of appetizers, entree dishes, and desserts, and be sure to ask the originator of the recipe if directions are unclear, including instructions written in "old-timey" English. For example, women of our grandmother's generation listed butter as "Oleo" in their recipes! For an added touch of nostalgia, create each page of your cookbook by copying the original recipe card, so everyone can see the recipe as it was written, printed in the creator's handwriting. ("Grandma Marie used to have the prettiest penmanship!")

"But I don't cook!" you say. "Why should I put together a family cookbook?" Because someday you just might want to learn how! And even if you never do, it would make a great contribution simply for posterity's sake. Besides, there's probably at least one thing you cook that you could contribute to such a tasty tome. Here's an example:

NACHOS Á LA ERIN AND WENDY

1 large bag Doritos "nacho cheesier" chips
1 16-ounce can of Cheez Whiz

1. Open bag of Doritos and pour desired amount of chips into bowl.
2. Unscrew lid of Cheez Whiz.
3. Dip chip into Cheez Whiz and eat.
4. Repeat until entire bowl of chips is gone.

Serving Suggestion:
Serve with Sam Adams beer while watching reruns of "The Simpsons."

 Ladies, Start Your Engines!

✳ Recipes don't have to be complicated to be good. Include lots of easy recipes—for dips and drinks, for example—for the "culinarily challenged" in your clan.

✳ If you're photocopying the book, include photos of the recipe's originator for added appeal.

✳ For more great tips, check out "Meals and Memories" on the Carlo Press website at www.carlopress.com.

117

Ladies, Start Your Engines!

Learn how to race vintage cars at a local track.

Why not combine your love of collecting both speeding tickets and antiques into a fast-paced hobby like racing vintage cars? With the exception of a few nudie bars and private golf courses, there's hardly anyplace left that's untouched by women, and the racetrack is no exception. From Mustangs to MGs, Camaros to Corvettes, women are feeling the same thrill of putting the pedal to the metal that men have been experiencing for years, proving that the need for speed is more about the rush of adrenaline through the blood than testosterone.

Why not experience your share of the action by spending a day at the racetrack, learning the ropes while avoiding the wall? You don't need to own a hot rod; oftentimes you can "rent" cars at the track or take a test drive during an event that's open to the public.

Even if vintage cars aren't available, you may be able to take a spin in a NASCAR-type demo car. Of course, you won't be going two hundred miles per hour and you may have a professional driver in the car with you offering some words of wisdom, beads of sweat, and sincere prayers to the god of psycho women drivers, but just the thrill of speeding without looking in your mirror for blue lights will be worth it.

Some states even have women's race clubs. Call a local racetrack or check on-line for an organization that's accepting beginners. Don't be

> "Have you ever noticed . . . anybody going slower than you is an idiot, and anyone going faster than you is a maniac?"
> —George Carlin

surprised to see ladies of all ages, races, and professions. Defying the speed limit and showing off your classic car are hardly interests limited by stereotypes. Some of the women may be great-grandmothers, beauticians, professors, or full-time moms. Some will own their cars, some will "borrow" their husbands', some may even be leasing theirs (just don't tell the dealership!).

Check out a women's race event to see what it's all about. You may decide it's not for you, but then again you may find yourself being drawn to the idea of living a real-life video game.

Be cautious, though. Racing cars can be contagious and the thrill could carry over into your everyday life. Check with your auto dealer to make sure your Pinto won't explode over fifty miles per hour, and the next time you rev your engine in an attempt to peel out as soon as the light turns green, make sure the lady in the car next to you isn't a cop, your mother, or a seventy-year-old grandmother in a V-8.

 Ladies, Start Your Engines!

✳ To get more info, contact Rocky Mountain Vintage Racers at 970-586-6366 or visit their website: www.rmvr.com.

✳ For fast-paced reading, pick up a copy of *NASCAR: The Definitive History of America's Sport* by Michael Hembree or *Women in Racing* by Michael Benson.

118

Excuse Me, but Your Pores Are Showing

Spend a day at a Native American sweat lodge.

Ever wonder why Pocahontas was so beautiful and serene? Long before the days of psychotherapy and Clearisil, Native Americans were tapping into Mother Nature's mind and body medicine chest: the sweat lodge. Forgo the expensive spa facials and headshrinker's bills; they are no match for what could be considered the world's cheapest and most effective homeopathic beauty regime.

Take a step back in time and spend a day at a Native American sweat lodge, cleansing your mental, emotional, and physical impurities in little more than a towel and a smile. Like a fine wine (or a six-pack of Old Milwaukee for you beer-guzzlin' tough chicks), your skin needs to breathe. Give it some room! With the possible exception of some ChapStick, your skin should be naked when you enter the lodge. Likewise, your mind and heart should be open, letting go of all those negative, spirit-clogging thoughts and emotions. You'll be amazed at the sense of calm you feel while steaming your pores open until they're the size of Malibu Barbie's pool.

The concept is hardly new, but despite its long history, few take advantage of the free (or relatively cheap) alternative beauty regime. Go figure! Women will pay hundreds of dollars to have their face steamed, popped, scrubbed, and peeled by a stranger whose name they can't pronounce, but they're uncomfortable

> "Beauty is only skin deep, and the world is full of thin-skinned people."
> —Richard Armour

sitting in a tent full of steam and strangers for fear that someone will think they're "one of those loony New Agers."

Let's say you've got a hot date coming up but you're caught in the destructive cycle wherein the more you worry about it, the more your face breaks out, and the more your face breaks out, the more you worry about the date. FAHGETABOUTIT! Plan a day trip to your nearby hot house and let the steam do the work! Within no time your potential dating disaster will become a thing of the past as your skin gives in to the luxury of a day without its usual annoying tag-along, Maybelline. Even Mr. Dreamboat will be forgotten as you contemplate the higher meaning of life.

Your trip to the sweat lodge is guaranteed to leave you with a refreshed spirit, revitalized energy, and even renewed interest in your hot date. Perhaps he'll notice the change in you: the glowing skin, the serene smile, the tightened pores, and the new sense of calm.

Ladies, Start Your Engines!

- Get firsthand opinions on sweat lodges from various sources on-line.
- Learn more about what to expect with *Native American Healing in the 21st Century*, a video by Rich-Heape Films Inc.
- Read before you bead (sweat beads, that is). Pick up a copy of Joseph Bruchac's (Abenaki) *The Native American Sweat Lodge, History and Legends.*

119

Foaming at the Mouth . . . of the River

Go white-water rafting.

"Up a creek without a paddle" is hardly a phrase reserved for the times when you're stuck on a blind date with a guy who cites his favorite movie as *Beavis and Butthead Do America*. While clichés tend to originate from real-life situations, the above mentioned is one you'd probably rather experience figuratively.

Of course, how will you know unless you take the plunge? Why not mix yourself a tall, cool glass of excitement with a splash of river water thrown in for good measure? (Shaken, not stirred, of course.) White-water rafting and canoeing are two of the true adventures that the "common folk" can take part in without being particularly physically fit. Even those with an affinity for a daily roll of cookie dough can enjoy the Lewis and Clark life with virtually no hindrances. Think of it as one of those kiddie rides where you have to meet the minimum requirements to ride. If you can fit into the life jacket you can ride the white waves, or even just paddle around in a creek.

There's no need for superior paddling skills, either. If you go white-water rafting, your group will probably consist of at least one expert oarsman, yelling out directions to those of you who are rowing—or valiantly attempting to keep your paddles in the water. Sure, your arms will get tired, but with the current doing most of the work, you'll probably only be steering the raft, not propelling it.

"Call on God, but row away from the rocks."
—**Native American proverb**

※

If you canoe, you can choose a mere trickle of water and take your time without having to fight a current.

Think no one will believe your tall tales of the waterworld? Many of today's rafting companies offer the option to have your picture taken midride. A photo taken from a bridge will capture the true excitement, fear, or exhilaration you're feeling as you pass underneath with your clan of fellow newbies. Don't worry about getting caught off guard. You won't have time to pick your nose or fix your wedgie.

Costs for trips can vary greatly, depending on the location and the length of your excursion. In some states, a half day of white-water rafting can cost as little as $12.00 per person. Canoeing is usually an inexpensive activity no matter where you live. Tourist stops, such as the Chamber of Commerce, tourist information, or rest areas, often carry pamphlets that contain coupons for day trips, especially if there's more than one rafting company near you and they need to compete for your business.

Most important, dive in with a sense of adventure and leave your vanity at home, especially if you choose the white-water voyage. As much as you'd like to look good in that photo from the bridge, don't count on it. People have been known to exit the raft bone dry, but your chances of being one of them are slim to none. Plan on bringing home a picture of yourself more closely resembling a drowned rat than a hip city slicker. Of course, you can always pull the picture out to abruptly put an end to that next horrible blind date.

 Ladies, Start Your Engines!

✴ For an experience that doesn't require a towel, check out *The Complete Whitewater Rafter* by Jeff Bennett or *Top-Rated River Adventures, Canoeing, Kayaking and Rafting in North America* by Maurice Valerio (photographer) and Allison C. Mickens (editor).

✴ Be sure to wear a life jacket. Just because you won a swimming trophy when you were ten doesn't mean that you can go without a life preserver.

120

Dónde Está la Cerveza?

Learn to speak a second (or third) language.

Despite the insistence of every cheesy pseudo-Casanova who manages to corner you on the dance floor with his bad shoes and even worse breath, the universal language of love won't get you very far in life. Speaking Spanish, Chinese, or even Russian, however, may be enough to net you a very high-paying job, a career with plenty of free travel, or just a very cool exotic lover.

Of course, there's a chance you may not get to use your new skill as often as you would like, but just learning the language can be both fun and empowering. You'll be able to actually understand what you're singing in your shower rendition of "O Sole Mio," and you'll be able to order the fancy entrees at a French bistro without the waiter's usual eye roll. "I'll have the cream bruley and a glass of the savignone blank."

Ditto with that hot Latino who sits beside you in Spanish 301. What's that cutie doing in here anyway, besides messing up the grade curve?! Perhaps your grasp of the native tongue will be impressive enough to win you an invitation to that hip new salsa club where the dance floor is so hot you can fry plantains on it. Ay Carumba! El tango es muy caliente!

Even Russian, with its throaty consonants and hard vowels, can sound sexy when coming from the right person. Remember all those Bond girls from the '60s? What better way to do your part for

> "I love Americans, but not when they try to talk French. What a blessing it is that they never try to talk English."
>
> – Saki (H. H. Munro)

world peace than to court a sexy Soviet hardbody who's only in town for the two-week Mr. Universe competition? Who needs more time than that to work your American Girl magic?

Have your heels become stuck to the same rung on the corporate ladder? Leave your Gucci pumps behind in search of a more worldly pair of climbing shoes with a second (or third) language beefing up your resume. As a second-place candidate for that kick-ass job in Japan you may be able to up the ante with a weeklong intensive language program. Why not clinch the deal by taking your boss to a Japanese restaurant and ordering all the food in Japanese? You'll knock the socks off the waiter and the indecision off your boss's mind.

Whatever language you choose to study, keep your newly acquired skills sharp with the "use it or lose it" frame of mind. Read Grecian poetry. Go to an Italian opera. Spend the weekend in Quebec or fly to Mexico for your birthday. Listen to the Latino radio station that you always flip past while searching for your Top 40 American pop. Saunter up to that Cuban cutie and ask his name in your sexiest senorita voice. Just be sure to check your breath before you corner him on the dance floor.

 Ladies, Start Your Engines!

* From books to cassettes to CD-ROMs, a range of useful language-learning tools are available on-line or at your local bookstore.

* Try reading any number of language-specific titles in the Teach Yourself series—for example, *Teach Yourself: Italian Language, Life, and Culture*.

* Or for you techies, look for 51 Languages of the World on CD-ROM from Transparent Language.

* You can listen and learn with audiocassettes like *Drive-in Chinese*. These are great for in your car or at home.

121

Green Eggs and Hamlet

Read to a group of kids at a library or bookstore.

If reading is fundamental, reading to kids must be fundamentally empowering! We're not talking about the works of Wordsworth or Shakespeare, but more likely *Horton Hears a Who!* or the Berenstain Bears. You can choose your childhood favorite or pick a new release from the children's book bestseller list.

Don't worry about trying to hold the interest of a room full of kids. Even the most select listener will tune in to hear the rhymes of Dr. Seuss or the adventures of Harry Potter! What child doesn't want to travel to distant lands, make friends with a talking animal, or have tea with a real-life fairy?

Check with your local library or bookstore for designated story times and offer up your storytelling services. Stores that specialize in children's books will probably have regularly scheduled readings already set up. Just add your name to the list and show up! You don't even have to bring (or buy, for that matter) your own book. Just show up with plenty of time to pick one out because the choices are endless and you don't want to keep a room full of eager preschoolers waiting.

How 'bout adding a little flair to your story time by dressing as a character in the book? Try any of the following to guarantee a roomful of intent ears:

* Squeeze into your old prom dress and sprinkle some glitter

> "A classic is a book which people praise and don't read."
> —**Mark Twain**

onto a pair of thrift-store pumps in order to effectively tell the glamorous tale of *Cinderella*, complete with a feminist slant. "And then Cinderella declined the prince's proposal of marriage, opting instead to hold herself responsible for her own happiness and financial security through spiritual awareness and a wide dispersement of midcap mutual fund investments. Any questions?"

✳ Don a red coat and cap and recite *Little Red Riding Hood*. Watch the eyes widen as you feign terror as Corporate American Male declares that his espresso-stained incisors are "all the better to eat you with." Um, excuse me, sir, but that's "all the better with which to eat you—you ended your sentence in a preposition."

✳ Remember *Little House on the Prairie*? Yeah, yeah—it was a TV show, but it was also a series of books. Rent a costume from the turn of the century and show up with some interesting tidbits about the era to share. "Back then, women did all the cooking, cleaning, child-rearing, teaching, and all-around crap work for little appreciation and no pay. Luckily, times have changed."

If you can't charm a gaggle of young'uns, don't even bother going to that cocktail party full of adults. The kids may seem like a tough crowd at first, but once you help them into a world with no boundaries, they'll latch onto you like a leech. Kids like adults who actually pay them some attention, so you might as well get used to being the belle of the ball. Besides, you may never get out of the prom dress.

 Ladies, Start Your Engines!

✳ Not sure what kids are reading today? Fall back on any of these classics:
- *The Story of Babar, the Little Elephant* by Jean De Brunhoff
- *Just So Stories* by Rudyard Kipling
- *The Complete Tales of Winnie-the-Pooh* by A. A. Milne
- *A Hatful of Seuss: Five Favorite Dr. Seuss Stories* by Dr. Seuss

122

Rollin' with the Homegirls

Spend a Saturday night roller-skating at a nearby rink.

Does the phrase "boogie with a briefcase" ring a bell? If you ate, slept, 253
and drank on roller skates in the '70s, it should. That song seems to
capture the pure ecstasy of roller-skating. But, since you're more likely
to be struck by lightning than hear it on your favorite radio station,
why not re-create the same great feeling by spending a Saturday night
at the roller rink!

For less than the cost of a movie, you can skate circles around novice
elementary schoolers with a vengeance for recapturing your own lost
youth. Just let them try to catch you as you whip by, with prepubescent
hormone-reeking wind at your back and the sound of Top 40 teeny-
bopper beats in your ear.

Unless you were a klutz twenty years ago, don't worry about top-
pling off your fluorescent wheels. Roller-skating is like riding a bike;
you'll most likely find your groove in the first five minutes. Reclaim
your title as the reigning rollerqueen of Ridgedale Elementary, even if
no one over twelve is there to bear witness.

Of course, your roller routine to "Xanadu" may earn you more than
points from the make-believe judge's panel (which originally consisted
of John Travolta, Cheryl Tiegs, and the Six Million Dollar Man). Expect
a few stares, pointing fingers, and giggles
(and perhaps even a few flash bulbs) as
you finesse your best backwards-reverse-
superduper-double hustle. Today's kids

> Roller skates were invented
> by American James Plimpton
> in 1863.

are too spoiled to understand the difficulty of a dance move that doesn't include a massive butt jiggle or a shoulder pop.

Still got your old Greenie Meanies hanging in the shed? Why not pull them out and give them to one of the girls at the rink who seems a sure bet to follow in your footsteps? You'll know her when you see her. She'll be the lone skater weaving in and out of her friends with a smile on her face and a Donna Summer beat in her ride. If she's got rentals on her feet it's probably not by choice. She may not be able to afford her own pair and yours might be just her size!

You could also hang onto your skates in hope that someday you'll be able to pass them on to your own daughter or niece. But there's always a chance that by the time she's old enough to skate, the new craze will be jet-propelled roller wings or invisible foot attachments. On the other hand, she may want to wax nostalgic with Mom's old skates—just to cause a stir with her friends and earn her the title of a true eccentric. Or maybe she'll wear them for Make Fun of Your Mother Day.

It could be worse. She could be wearing your prom dress.

 Ladies, Start Your Engines!

✳ Be sure to wear good socks! Two pairs even. You can always take one pair off if your feet start sweating and you'll be decreasing your chances of developing a nasty blister.

✳ Call ahead to make sure there are no themes. You don't want to show up in regular clothes if everyone else is decked out in '60s attire for Hippies night.

✳ Find out if you can wear rollerblades instead. If you've got your own pair, it'll save you the rental fee.

123

Shooting Blanks

Release some stress by blasting strangers in a game of laser tag.

It's not like anyone's disputing your claim that your boss is a tyrant. Nor are they praising the positive attributes of your neighbor, who's been threatening to barbecue your dog if it poops on his lawn one more time. Still, having everyone on your side isn't always enough to eradicate your outright disgust and frustration toward the jerks who continually plague your otherwise great life. And since spontaneous combustion is rare, you can't afford to move cross-country, and poisoning their coffee is illegal (remember the movie *9 to 5*?), you'll just have to find an alternative form of decompression.

How about trying your hand at laser tag? It's a safe, inexpensive, and totally legal form of entertainment, and you'll feel an instant fix when you pretend the prey du jour is that special someone who makes your daily existence a living hell.

Here's how it works. You'll be strapped into a lightweight vest to gauge the number of hits you receive, and your "laser light" (the industry tries not to use the word *gun*) will track the number of hits you make on other players. You'll be briefed on the rules then led into a big maze, complete with black lights, ramps, tunnels, and loud music. The key is to earn points under your self-determined code name while avoiding hits from other players. A hit will typically give you a ten-second delay, during which time your laser light won't work, but you also won't

> "Never insult seven men when all you're packing is a six-shooter."
> —Zane Gray

be able to accumulate hits from other players. It's best to use that time to hide from the pithy little creatures who will be scrambling to tag you as soon as you're back in the game.

Worried you'll be up against a bunch of militant eighteen-year-old boys who plan their work schedules around their paint ball tournaments? Don't be. You'll probably be surprised to learn that the ages of participants range from eight to eighty-eight. Whether or not you'll be *pleasantly* surprised is another story. Preteens tend to have a lot of pent-up aggression due to hormonal surges and unresolved issues with their math teachers. Don't expect them to be gentle on you just because you're a first-timer.

Being a first-timer has its advantages, though, because you have an untapped source of anger to draw from. Consider yourself a kamikaze representing all underpaid, underappreciated women, zapping anyone within eyesight who even slightly resembles your boss, neighbor, or that lady at the Petite Boutique who asked you if you were there to buy a gift for someone else.

Maybe you can make laser tag a regular part of your day. You might want to see if they have a frequent user card—then you could actually invite your boss the next time you go.

 Ladies, Start Your Engines!

✳ Although you don't have to wear sneakers, definitely wear low, comfortable shoes. You'll be sneaking around in the dark and the clickity clack of hard-soled shoes will give away your coordinates for sure!

✳ Wear dark clothes if you're serious about your game. Light colors, especially white, will stand out in the fluorescent glow, making you an easy target.

✳ Call ahead to make sure there are no private parties.

124

Your Move, Miss Daisy

Challenge a nearby nursing home's reigning chess champion to a game.

Think you've got what it takes to retain your title as chess queen of your neighborhood's most brilliant (and geeky) minds? Why not take the ultimate test by challenging the reigning champ of an area nursing home? You may be able to move your pieces faster, but the old-timers have the advantage of years of wisdom and perhaps thousands of games.

If you find that your senior facility of choice doesn't have a reigning queen or king, why not create your own chess championship? Start by clearing the concept with the director and the staff, then post a sign-up sheet and let the round robin begin! Don't forget to scribble your own name into the play-offs. Assuming you'll make it into the final four is hardly fair. (What happened to your modesty?) You may want to find out just how good these blue-haired guys and dolls are before talking the talk. Better to get your butt kicked in an early round when no one is watching than to have the entire group of residents and staff watch while Mr. Finkeldorf wipes the floor with your smug little grin. Ouch!

If your title as chess champ was merely a rumor started by your devious older brother who wanted to portray you as a geek in high school or a facade to cover your feelings of inadequacy as a less-than-stellar player, why not admit your weakness and seek out a mentor to

> "The mistakes are all waiting to be made."
>
> —Chessmaster Savielly Grigorievitch Tartakower

teach you the ropes? There's bound to be at least one top dog at the home who's willing to pass on his or her legacy of kick-ass strategies.

If you're somewhere between expert and novice, the best thing you can do to build your skills is to practice, practice, practice. And since your friends have made their opinions of chess quite clear through their rolled eyes and deep sighs whenever you break out the board, you should be thrilled to find a partner who is almost as eager to play as you are. You may even find that several of the residents love chess, leading you to actually schedule your matches in order to accommodate your long list of challengers. You've struck the mother, or rather "grandmother," lode, my dear, with a never-ending lineup of ready and willing opponents.

Your friends, of course, will be happy to hear that you're getting your fill of the game *before* they come over to hang out Saturday night.

 Ladies, Start Your Engines!

Get a leg up on your opponent with these fun titles:

✻ *Chess for Beginners* (Fireside Chess Library) by Israel A. Horowitz and Sol Horowitz

✻ *101 Questions on How to Play Chess* by Fred Wilson

✻ *The ABCs of Chess: Invaluable, Detailed Lessons for Players of All Levels* by Bruce Pandolfini

I Wear My Sunglasses at Night

Find out just how good you've got it when you hear someone croon the blues.

The word on the street is that you're feeling pretty down. Maybe it's the result of the five pounds of chocolate you ate before your last period. Maybe it's the fact that your cat ran away because you gave her 1 percent milk instead of her usual skim. Or maybe the bagger at your grocery store just called you "Ma'am" for the first time when asking you if you needed help with your bag.

Whatever your excuse, you need to stop feeling sorry for yourself! There are plenty of people who are far worse off than you. If you don't believe it, check out blues night at an out-of-the-way joint and perk up your spirits as you learn why "down and out" and "Beverly Hills" never should have been in the same sentence, much less a movie title.

Don your best "fitting in" outfit—namely, a pair of reflective sunglasses, so you can stare without getting your ass kicked, and a thick cigar to hide in the smoke at your private table. Be sure to request a seat near the back or at the bar so you can make a nonchalant entrance—many of the blues clubs have their own "regular" crowd and you're not part of it—and a quick exit if you suddenly feel the need to go give thanks for how well everything is going in your life.

Indeed, some of the songs you'll hear are sure to move you to tears, if you can actually figure out what the old men are mumbling behind their guitars. Key phrases to listen for

> "Sounds like the blues are composed of feeling, finesse, and fear."
> —Billy Gibbons

include "my old lady left me," "ain't got no job," and "I can see the bottom of the bottle already." Although it's probably best not to try to sing along, feel free to close your eyes and hum a few bars inside your head.

You'll probably hear a few "Mmmhhm. Oh yeah. Sing it, brother!"s, the blues version of the ever-popular Clintonesque, "I feel your pain," but until you frequent the joint enough for the bartender to remember your drink (anything that ends in "straight up" will help you fit in), don't try adding your own verbal outburst to the list of amenlike affirmations. Just sit back and enjoy the company of someone else's misery. You'll probably leave feeling confident enough to head back to that grocery store and make that bag boy carry your one bag—of skim milk and chocolate—out to your car.

 ## Ladies, Start Your Engines!

✳ Preview some of the blues clubs during the day. Ask the waitress or bartender to describe the night crowd and music.

✳ Call ahead to see if there's a cover charge or dress code.

✳ Bring cash. Not all clubs take checks and credit cards.

✳ Ask a friend who enjoys the blues to recommend a favorite hot spot.

✳ Not sure where to start? Pick up any of these blues classics to get a head start:
- *The Best of Friends* by John Lee Hooker
- *His Best 1947–55* by Muddy Waters
- *The Essential Etta James*
- *Greatest Hits* by Stevie Ray Vaughan
- *The Quintessential Billie Holiday Volume 2: 1936*
- *Live at the Regal* by B. B. King